I Don't Know What to Say

'I'm very grateful for Robert Buckman's book. It deals, with honesty, love and deep practicality, with a subject that the vast majority of people prefer to pretend does not exist. But death is a fact of life and it is one with which we must all come to terms. With Dr Buckman's help readers can come to terms not only with the death of people they care about but with their own eventual deaths. And that is something for which, as I say, I personally am very grateful.'

Claire Rayner

'There is much to receive as well as to give in being with those who are dying or bereaved. Here is a book to help us meet in this demanding and rewarding area of communication and, indeed, at many other times. Its ease of style and clarity of presentation will help many, both among the general public and professionals. We are all in Dr Buckman's debt once again.'

Dame Cicely Saunders, DBE, FRCP, FRCS

'Most useful and compassionate.'

Jack Jones

Born in 1948, Dr Robert Buckman qualified in 1972 from Cambridge University and University College Hospital, London. He became interested in cancer medicine in 1975 and went to the Royal Marsden Hospital in London where he trained in cancer medicine including laboratory research, leading to a PhD.

During this time, he became interested in wider aspects of medicine and health, and from 1977 he has appeared regularly in science programmes for Yorkshire Television. In 1981 he became co-presenter with Miriam Stoppard of 'Where There's Life . . .' In 1986 he completed a series of six programmes entitled 'The Buckman Treatment', films looking at health care issues. A second series will be shown in the autumn of 1988.

In the last few years, in his hospital and teaching practice, he has concentrated on various aspects of the doctor–patient relationship, particularly with respect to breaking bad news and supportive care of the dying and their families.

Besides these interests, he maintains an active involvement in laboratory research and undergraduate teaching and also finds time to contribute a weekly humorous column to *Punch*.

Dr Buckman now lives in Toronto, Canada, where he is a full-time medical oncologist (cancer specialist) and Assistant Professor at the Toronto Bayview Cancer Centre at the Sunnybrook Hospital, University of Toronto.

I Don't Know What to Say

How To Help and Support Someone who is Dying

by Dr Robert Buckman

with contributions by
Ruth Gallop RN & Reverend John Martin

PAPERMAC

First published 1988 in paperback by
PAPERMAC
a division of Macmillan Publishers Limited
4 Little Essex Street London WC2R 3LF and Basingstoke

Associated companies in Auckland, Delhi, Dublin, Gaborone, Hamburg, Harare, Hong Kong, Johannesburg, Kuala Lumpur, Lagos, Manzini, Melbourne, Mexico City, Nairobi, New York, Singapore, and Tokyo

British Library Cataloguing in Publication Data
Buckman, Rob
    I don't know what to say: how to help and
    support someone who is dying.
    1. Terminal care
    I. Title
    362.1'75   R726.8

ISBN 0-333-45737-4
    0-333-46983-6 Pbk

Reprinted 1988 (twice)

Typeset by Wyvern Typesetting Ltd, Bristol

Printed and bound by Richard Clay Ltd, Bungay, Suffolk

To Robin and Prue Skynner for teaching me so much

Contents

Part Three: Practicalities

Preface

In writing this book I have drawn on the skills and expertise of two people – Ruth Gallop and John Martin. We wrote it together, not just because we all share a professional involvement with terminally ill people, but also because of our respective backgrounds. John Martin is a chaplain with a wide experience in street ministry. He spent several years helping people on the fringes of society before he focused on the care of the terminally ill and took up his present post as hospital chaplain at the cancer centre where I work. Ruth Gallop has trained both as a nurse and as a psychotherapist but her experience goes far beyond her training. Her first husband, Leslie, died before his thirtieth birthday of a rare tumour after two years of illness, leaving her with a young son. That happened more than fifteen years ago while I was a medical student, and the many conversations I had with both Ruth and Leslie changed my view of medicine. It is largely as a result of what I learned from them that I decided to specialise in cancer medicine. Ruth has brought to this book the insights of a talented psychotherapist, together with those of someone who has been through the experience of a deep loss. She survived that loss and rebuilt her family and life, and has achieved remarkable personal and professional growth as a result.

My own experience was with an auto-immune disease (in which

the body's defence system overreacts and attacks the body itself), which nearly paralysed me for two years, and at one stage threatened my life. It taught me many things that I should have known before. As a patient I learned the value of the sympathy and support that distinguishes good doctors from ordinary ones.

Many other people have helped me, directly and indirectly. Dr Eve Wiltshaw showed me that a doctor can be an expert and be humane at the same time. Robin and Prue Skynner taught me the central elements of therapeutic dialogue. Reverend Robert Hunt helped me with many aspects of ethical and spiritual issues.

In putting this book together, we have tried to use as much as we could of what we have learned from our patients and their families. Supporting someone who is dying is always demanding, often tiring, and sometimes exhausting, but it is one of the most valuable things that one human being can do for another. For everyone who takes on this important job, I hope that *I Don't Know What to Say* will be of real and practical help.

If there are ways in which you think this book could be improved, or if you have ideas that might help other people, we'd be glad to hear from you.

Robert Buckman
November 1987

Who is 'the Patient'?

Throughout this book I use the word 'patient' to mean 'the person who has the illness'. It's unfortunate that there isn't a better word, because 'patient' is a word with overtones of hospitals and doctors and it does sound rather clinical. But it's the best word we've got at the moment. Recently some authors have started talking about, for example, people with cancer as PWCs – which sounds even more clinical and less personal, and is a thoroughly retrograde step.

I need to stress that when I use the word I never forget that every patient is a person. All patients are people before they become ill, during their illness and afterwards in our minds and memories. In my view there is a central formula:

$$patient = person + disease$$

and even though the word 'patient' doesn't convey much to do with real people, it's simply the best way of telling you which person I'm talking about.

Introduction

I bumped into James in the lobby of the hospital. I was a junior medical student and my family and James' family had been friends for as long as I could remember. Now James' mother had been admitted to hospital and was found to have cancer of the kidney. James was sitting downstairs in the lobby looking miserable and blank. I asked him whether he was on his way up to see his mother. 'I've been sitting here for half an hour,' he said. 'I want to go and see her, but I'm stuck. I don't know what to say.'

As I sat with him, I realised that if it had been my mother upstairs in the hospital bed I wouldn't have known what to say either. And as I went on through medical school and into medical practice I realised that thousands of people don't know what to say – and that includes some doctors. Most of us don't know what to say because nobody has told us. I decided to write this book for James, for myself and for everybody else who has a friend or relative facing the end of his life and wants to help but doesn't know how.

I've written this book with two purposes in mind: first, to explain the process of dying and death in enough detail to demystify it for friends or family of the dying person; and second, to give practical hints and advice to help those close to the dying person to be of greater support to the patient.

In this book I'm going to explain in plain English what it is that so often goes wrong between patient and family. I'll show how misunderstandings and obstacles arise, and how they can be dealt with – or at least how the problems they cause can be minimised. Reading this book will help you to understand the emotions that you may be feeling, which are often complex, and also the emotions that the dying person is feeling. You'll find that there are many different ways to side-step the blocks and bridge the communication gaps.

It will also help you to understand what's going on and how you can help. It won't abolish the pain and the difficulty, but it'll make them easier to bear. In that respect, it's like a book on pregnancy and childbirth: the more you know about what's happening and what's likely to happen, the less anxious and frightened you are. But no book can shorten a pregnancy or make a birth totally painless.

In some ways, the Big Secret is simply that there's no Big Secret. All that is needed is a desire to help and an understanding of what's going on. I assume that you're reading this book in the first place because you have that desire, and I hope the book itself will give you the understanding. It will also give you permission – permission to feel the way you do feel, permission to say things that need to be said (and shouldn't be left unsaid), and permission to help and support in the way you really want to.

You're not alone

If the image of James feeling nervous and 'stuck' because he didn't know what to say to his mother strikes a chord with you, then the first thing you need to know is that you're not alone. Most people don't know how to help, not because of their own failings or inadequacies but because serious illness and the threat of death are very powerful forces. They can – and often do – tear relationships apart, separating and isolating the patient from family and friends and making everybody confused and embarrassed. As a doctor specialising in cancer medicine, as a family member, and to a limited extent as a patient, I've seen hundreds of marriages, relationships and friendships split apart by illness and death. But, what's more important, I've seen how things can often be made better in relatively easy ways – ways that I shall be describing later.

Of course nothing you read here can take away the pain of losing your friend – only the completing of grief will do that – but what you read will help you understand the emotions and the reactions that both you and the patient may experience. This understanding will help you deal with the confusion, the awkward silences and the subtle resentments that get in the way and stop you from helping.

Before we go any further I think I ought to come clean and say that I don't believe in the mystique of death. I don't believe that death is a fine and wonderful thing in itself. I don't see it as a white light, a secret garden, a butterfly coming out of a cocoon or any other concrete image, however beautiful. Some people do have strong images like these which give them inner peace and tranquillity and allow them to accept dying with little difficulty. But for many people, that kind of inner support isn't there – which is one of the main reasons why this book is needed.

To me, dying is the ending of a life and it is almost always sad, even though it may be an end to physical suffering and be a natural relief.

This means that you won't find a magic formula in this book that will miraculously ease your pain and convert the loss of your friend into a joyous transition. There are no instant solutions here, but only a way of working out what the most important questions are, and ways of arriving at solutions that work best for your friend and for yourself.

In beginning to sort out these questions, it is important to realise that a lot of the anxiety and confusion surrounding the subject of dying has its beginnings in our society – in the way we are all brought up and taught about the world. I'm going to start with a brief look at those factors that make this subject awkward for us before we are even fully aware of it.

Why talking about dying is difficult

We live in a society in which dying is not part of the business of living. Phrases describing dying as 'the last taboo' or 'the new obscenity' are clichés, but they tell us something about the way we think. They tell us that we think of death as something alien, something outside the bounds of daily life, something unnatural.

Now we all really know that death is not unnatural. We know that all life ends in death and that (another cliché) it's the one thing that we can all be absolutely certain of. We know this in our minds, but as a society we've decided not to acknowledge it or talk about it in a natural way. We pretend that it isn't really there.

So what? Why should we acknowledge death?

Well, acknowledgement is important because denial makes things very difficult for friends and family. When a person is dying, his friends and family can no longer deny the reality of his death, but if they have not previously acknowledged its existence they are now ill-prepared to face it. The denial of death creates a barrier between the dying person and the rest of society, so that the person facing death seems to be stepping outside the boundaries of our society before he has taken leave of life. He becomes isolated and set apart from his friends by the conventions of our society at the very time that he most needs our support.

Why has dying become isolated from daily life? The major causes seem to be these:

- our elders rarely die at home
- we have very high expectations of health and life
- we depend utterly on experts during illness
- our society places high emphasis on material values
- there is a current crisis in spiritual direction

Let me say clearly that I am not condemning these things as wrong. I don't happen to believe that our society is totally self-destructive or evil, nor do I believe that everything was wonderful and perfect a century ago. All I am saying is that the way we lead our daily lives in Western society today makes it very difficult to face dying with equanimity.

Let me start with the way in which death is excluded from most people's experience as they grow up. Only a few decades ago, when the extended family was more common – when grandparents lived in the same home as their grandchildren – it was quite common for elderly relatives to die at home, surrounded by their families. This meant that children were quite likely to have their first experience of a death when they were quite young, and, more important, were surrounded by their own parents and brothers and sisters. In other words, dying would be seen by these younger children as part of family living – they would think it was natural. Sometimes the rosy ideal of an elderly person gently fading away surrounded by the nearest and dearest wasn't achieved. But even when there was pain and trauma it would occur inside the family circle where there could be support, so that however unpleasant it might be, it would still be part of growing up.

Things aren't like that any more. Most adults have not seen anyone die at home, and this is one reason death appears to be something foreign.

A second reason why dying has been set apart from everyday experience is the expectation of a healthy life that we have nowadays. Every time the newspapers carry news of a major breakthrough in medicine – whether it's a heart transplant, marrow grafting, interleukin-2 or anything else – our attitudes to illness and death change further. Each time we tend to think, 'Right, they've fixed that – what next?' At the back of our minds, perhaps, we're hoping that 'they' are going to come up with a cure for old age – and preferably before we get old ourselves. Of course this attitude isn't bad in itself. It's good that we greet advances in health care positively, even though many of the most public advances may affect only a few people and may not prolong the average life expectancy at all. But each time we see the frontiers of health pushed forward a little bit, each time we hear that a disease which was previously known to be incurable is now treatable, we start thinking that soon there must be a cure for everything. In other words, we move closer to thinking of death as something that could be prevented for ever with just another little bit of technical know-how. Of course we know this isn't really true. We all know that there's no such thing as immortality, but each time the newspapers tell us of another 'miracle cure' it becomes that much easier to hope. And as our expectations of a healthy life increase, the thought of dying seems ever more alien and unnatural.

Third, illness and dying seem to have become the province of experts. This, too, is quite logical. Looking after sick people is often a business that requires technical knowledge, and a lot of it goes on in hospitals full of expensive equipment and drugs. Again, there's nothing wrong with this. If it takes high-tech medicine to make a person better (however temporarily) then he should be in a high-tech environment where he can get what he needs. This usually creates no major difficulty while the patient is getting better, but tends to create serious problems at the point when he is no longer improving and begins the process of dying.

As long as the patient is in a high-tech curing phase, his family and friends seem to have little role to play in supporting him, and the illness becomes the exclusive business of the hospital and doctors. Then, when medical technology has nothing further to offer, the friends have lost their role and remain at a distance, often expecting more intervention from the doctors.

If doctors were as good at caring for dying patients as they are at looking after acute illnesses, there would be no problem. They would feel comfortable handing back some of the support of the dying person to the family. Often, however, the doctors are reluctant to accept the failure of their techniques to cure the patient. Thus, at the time when the friends and family could be of greatest value to the patient there is often a diffusion of responsibility in which the doctors realise that their own role is limited but feel uneasy about saying so openly. Inadvertently, the medical staff may become a dog-in-the-manger, unable to support the patient but equally unable to hand over to those who can.

None of this is intended as destructive criticism of the medical profession. As doctors, we do our best to be experts in treating patients, and it is sad that most of us have not been taught the additional skills required to support patients suffering from incurable diseases. Things are changing rapidly, however, and these skills are now included in many medical school curricula. It is very likely that the next generation of doctors will be more expert in relieving the symptoms of dying patients, and in involving the family and friends in their support.

Other reasons for our thinking about death as outside the normal business of life are those concerned with the way our society puts values on various aspects of our lives. Specifically, these reasons have to do with the materialist values of our society, and the spiritual crisis in which a large proportion of Western society finds itself.

Our society has been called a 'here and now' society, meaning that tremendous importance is attached to material values and success, however temporary they are. We are accustomed to assessing the worth and meaning of a life in material terms. I am not implying that materialism is intrinsically wrong or dangerous, but simply that it has a price: the more a society accepts material values as the standard by which a life is assessed, the more that society will undervalue human contacts and inter-relationships, and the more it will regard the end of life as fearsome and tragic. Any society that rates materialist values highly creates individuals who find the idea of death difficult. For them, life is fun, and death is the end of fun.

Another social cause of the estrangement of death from life is the way in which religion and spiritual values have changed. A few centuries ago, when there was little knowledge of the workings of the physical universe, it was easy to conjure up a strong image of God as a divine architect who controlled all events on earth and who would mete out rewards after death. As more and more knowledge accumulated about physical events previously considered 'eternal mysteries', so the role and the realm of God and religion have changed. Some religions now focus on personal faith, others have tried to retain older traditions and the values that go with them. Again, I am not saying that this is good or bad. I merely observe that many patients are not accustomed to strong spiritual influences in their daily lives, and cannot call on a lifelong faith to support them at the end.

These, then, are some of the most important social factors that make the subject of death generally difficult to talk about for all of us. But in this materialist way of summing up a life it's very easy to lose sight of a simple truth: death ends life but certainly doesn't rob it of meaning. I think we all need to be reminded that in our lives we affect and change the people closest to us. Those changes have a very considerable value, even if you can't add them up quickly and easily. For instance, I am not the same person that I would have been had I not met James, Ruth, John or the many others who have made a major impression on me. Some people even think of these changes as a form of immortality, which makes a lot of sense to me, and suggest that people who have died, or who are dying, do live on, in a way, by the changes that they have caused in those who survive them. You cannot make people remember you, even if you have a library or office-block named after you, but if you've altered the way people think, then some of the meaning of your life will survive after your death.

In summary, then, there are many causes of our society's view that death is something outside the mainstream of life and that, for all these reasons, we find that there are now barriers between Us, the bystanders, and Them, our friends who are facing death. I think it is very important to recognise that many of those barriers were not created by us individually and they are not our fault. Once you realise that you are struggling to overcome a block that society has put in your way, it gets a little easier to step round it. And that's what we shall be dealing with in the rest of this book.

PART ONE

Talking and Listening

1
Why Talk? Why Listen?

If talking to someone who is terminally ill is so difficult, why try it? Why is it worth doing and what can you achieve by talking with and listening to someone who is seriously ill?

In my experience, in giving support and easing distress, both the donor and the recipient are rewarded. These actions have worth and value because they strengthen your relationship with each other. They make a new bond between you at a time when, if you didn't talk to each other, the strain would otherwise separate you. Thus, if you *don't* talk to each other you run a serious risk of ending up as strangers at a time when you most need to be friends; if you *do* communicate with each other the reward is an enhanced relationship.

There are several important points about dialogue that may seem extremely obvious if you think about them when you are feeling calm and tranquil, but that are easily forgotten when you are under duress.

1. *Talking happens to be the best method of communication we have.* There are, of course, many different ways of communicating: kissing, touching, laughing, frowning, even not talking. (I'm reminded of the man who wanted to know why his wife hadn't spoken to him for three days and his psychotherapist replied,

'Perhaps she's trying to tell you something.') However, talking is the most efficient and the most *specific* way we have of communicating.

2. *Simply talking about distress helps to relieve it.* There are many reasons for us to talk. There are obvious ones, such as telling the children not to stick their fingers in the fan, telling a joke, asking about the results of the game or the horse-race and so on. But there are also less obvious reasons for talking, among which is the simple desire to be listened to. In many circumstances – particularly when things go wrong – people talk in order to get what is bothering them off their chests, and to be heard. You can see this quite often in the behaviour of children. If you have an argument with your child, you may hear him grumbling later to his teddy bear, or even telling the bear off in the way you told the child off. Now this is not exactly dialogue or conversation – it's one-way – but it serves a useful function. It releases a bit of pressure, and human beings can only stand so much pressure. There is a relief in talking, which means that there is relief that *you* can provide for a sick person by listening, and by simply *allowing* them to talk. This in turn means that you can help your friend even if you don't have all the answers.

In fact, simply doing 'good listening' (which will be described in the next chapter) is known to be effective *just by itself*. An interesting research study was conducted in the United States in which a number of totally untrained people were taught the simple techniques of good listening, and volunteer patients came to see them to talk about their problems. The listeners in this study were not allowed to say or do anything at all apart from nodding and saying 'I see,' or 'Tell me more.' They weren't allowed to ask questions of the patients, or say anything at all about the problems that the patients described. At the end of the hour, almost all the patients thought they had received very good therapy. Some even telephoned the 'therapists' to ask if they could see them again, and to thank them for the therapy. It is always worth remembering that *you don't have to have the answers – just listening to the questions will help*.

3. *Thoughts that a person tries to shut out will eventually do harm.* One of the arguments friends and family put forward in order to *avoid* talking to the patient is that talking about a fear or an anxiety might *create* that anxiety, even if it didn't exist before the conversation. In

other words, a friend might say to himself, 'If I ask my friend if he's worried about radiotherapy and he isn't worried about it, I might *make* him worried about it.' Well, that doesn't happen. There's very good evidence from studies done by psychologists talking to patients with terminal cancer that conversations between patients and their relatives and friends does not create new fears and anxieties. In fact, the opposite is true: *not* talking about a fear makes it bigger; those patients who have nobody to talk to have a higher incidence of anxiety and depression. Several other researchers have shown that when people are seriously ill one of their biggest problems is that people won't talk to them, and the feelings of isolation add a great deal to their burdens. In practice, a major anxiety occupying a patient's mind frequently makes it difficult for that patient to talk about anything at all.

Bottled-up feelings may cause damage because, in many cases, people are ashamed of their feelings – particularly of their fears and anxieties. They find that they are afraid of something but feel that they aren't 'supposed' to be, and so feel ashamed of themselves. One of the greatest services you can do for your friend is to hear his fears and stay close when you've heard them. By not backing away or withdrawing you show that you accept and understand them. This will in itself help to reduce the fear, and the shame, and help the patient get his sense of perspective back.

So, for all these reasons, you have everything to gain and nothing to lose by trying to talk to – and listen to – someone who's seriously ill. Despite this, it sometimes feels very awkward at the beginning, and it may seem as if the patient doesn't want to talk. If you are feeling nervous yourself, then you may not want to talk either. There are four major obstacles to free communication between you and the patient. These are:

The patient wants to talk	You don't
The patient doesn't want to talk	You do
The patient wants to talk but feels he ought not to	You don't know how to encourage him to talk
The patient *appears* not to want to talk but really *needs* to	You don't know what's best – and don't want to intervene if it makes things worse

In the rest of this book, I'm going to be showing you some ways of making yourself available for listening and talking without thrusting your offer down the patient's throat, and ways in which you can work out whether the patient needs to talk or doesn't. In the next chapter I shall explain some basic technicalities of listening that will make it easier for you.

2

Sensitive Listening

Good listening may appear simple, but in practice it is a very tricky art, and doctors are often as bad at it as anyone else. However, it is relatively easy to turn yourself into a responsive and sensitive listener by noting a few important details.

A lot depends on how you and your friend have talked with each other in the past. However much you improve your ability to listen, you will not necessarily change your friend's usual style of communication. If your friend was always easy to talk to and spoke about his feelings freely, then that's likely to continue now. If, however, he has always been a private and closed person, you will not make him a 'good talker' just by your becoming a good listener, and it is not realistic to hope for that kind of change. What you can do is give him an opportunity to air the things he's concerned about. On occasions that may make a big difference. Some people don't talk because their friends never really listen, and in times of crisis a good listener can create an atmosphere that's radically different. However, that doesn't happen with everybody or on every occasion, so it is important to avoid setting your expectations too high.

Basically, good listening can be divided into two parts: the physical part and the mental part. A lot of the most awkward communication gaps are caused by not knowing a few simple rules that encourage free conversation:

1. *Get the setting right.* The physical context is important, and it's worth getting the details correct from the start. Get comfortable, sit down, try to look relaxed (even if you don't feel it); try to signal the fact that you are there to spend some time (for instance, take your coat off!). Keep your eyes on the same level as the person you're talking to, and keep looking at her while she is talking. Keep within a comfortable distance of her. Generally, there should be one to two feet of space between you – a longer distance makes dialogue awkward and formal, and a shorter distance can make the patient feel hemmed in, particularly if she is in bed and is unable to back away. Try to make sure that there are no physical obstacles (desks, bedside tables and so on) between you. If the patient is in hospital and chairs are unavailable or too low, sitting on the bed is preferable to standing.

2. *Find out whether the patient wants to talk.* It may be that he is simply not in the mood to talk, or even that he doesn't want to talk to you that day. Try not to be offended if that's the case. If you're not sure what the patient wants you can always ask ('Do you feel like talking?'), which is always better than launching into a deep conversation ('Tell me about your feelings') if he is tired or has just been talking to someone else.

3. *Listen and show you're listening.* When the patient is talking, you should try to do two things: first, listen instead of thinking of what you're going to say next; and second, *show* that you're listening.

To listen properly, you must be thinking about what the patient is saying. You should not be rehearsing your reply (which would mean that you're anticipating what you think the patient is *about* to say, and not listening to what he *is* saying). This means you must try not to interrupt the patient. While she is talking, don't talk yourself but wait for her to stop speaking before you start. If she interrupts you while *you're* saying something, with a 'but . . .' or a 'I thought . . .' or something similar, you should stop and let her say what she wants.

4. *Encourage him to talk.* Good listening isn't just sitting there like a running tape-recorder. You can actually help the patient to talk about what's on his mind by encouraging him. Simple things work very well. Try nodding, or saying affirmative things like 'Yes,' 'I see,' or 'Tell me more.' This sounds simple but actually at times of

maximum stress it's the simple things you need to help things along.

You can also show that you're hearing – and listening – by repeating two or three words from the patient's last sentence. This really does help the talker to feel that his words are being taken on board. Actually when I teach medical students how to talk with patients I get them to try this word-repetition technique on their friends at home. They invariably report that it moves the conversation along and makes the listener suddenly appear more interested and involved.

You can also reflect back to the talker what you've heard, partly to check that you've got it right, and partly to show that you're listening and trying to understand. You can say things like 'So you meant that . . .' or 'If I've got that straight, you feel . . .' or even 'I hear you,' although that last one might sound a bit self-conscious if it isn't your usual style.

5. *Don't forget silence and non-verbal communication.* If someone stops talking it usually means that she is thinking about something painful or sensitive. Wait with her for a moment – hold her hand or touch her if you feel like it – and then ask her what she was thinking about. Don't rush it, even though silences at emotional moments do seem to last for years.

Another point about silences is that sometimes you may think, 'I don't know what to say'. On occasions, this may be because there isn't anything *to* say. If that's the case, don't be afraid to say nothing and just stay close. At times like that, a touch or an arm round the patient's shoulder can be of greater value than any words.

If your friend is tired, offer to sit by the bedside while he sleeps. Simply being there with him is a valuable means of support. Even if you are not saying anything, your presence is an antidote for loneliness.

6. *Don't be afraid to describe your own feelings.* You're allowed to say things like, 'I find this difficult to talk about,' or 'I'm not very good at talking about . . .' or even 'I don't know what to say.' Describing your emotions is valuable whatever they are.

7. *Make sure you haven't misunderstood.* If you are sure you understand what the patient means, you can say so. Responses such as, 'You sound very low,' or 'That must have made you very angry,' tell the patient that you've picked up the emotions he's been talking about or showing. But if you're not sure what the patient

means, then ask, 'What did you feel like?' 'What do you think of it?' 'How do you feel now?' Misunderstandings can arise if you make assumptions and are wrong. This happened to a colleague of mine, Peter, who is a family practitioner. He was looking after a middle-aged woman with a terminal illness. The patient was a lawyer and had been in hospital for several weeks before getting back to her home, weak and enfeebled. On one of Peter's visits to her at home she sighed and asked him, 'How long will it be?' Peter was just about to tell her that she would probably die within the next few weeks when he suddenly wondered whether she was really referring to her death. He hesitated and then asked her what she meant. She said, 'I meant how long will it be before I can get back to work and be in court again?' Peter sat with her for a long time and got her to talk about how she thought she was doing, and he only answered the question after a lot more preparation.

It's certainly advantageous when you instinctively pick up what the patient is feeling, but if you don't happen to do that, don't hesitate to ask. Something like, 'Help me to understand what you mean a bit more,' is quite useful.

8. *Don't change the subject.* If your friend wants to talk about how rotten he feels, let him. It may be difficult for you to hear some of the things he is saying, but if you can manage it then stay with him while he talks. If you find it too uncomfortable and think you just can't handle the conversation at that moment, then you should say so and offer to try to discuss it again later. Don't simply change the subject without acknowledging the fact that your friend has raised it.

9. *Don't give advice early.* Ideally, no one should give advice to anyone else unless it's asked for. However, this isn't an ideal world and quite often we find ourselves giving advice when we haven't quite been asked. Try not to give advice early in the conversation, because it stops dialogue. If you're bursting to give advice, it's often easier to use phrases like, 'Have you thought about trying . . .?' or (if you're a born diplomat) 'A friend of mine once tried . . .' These are both less bald than, 'If I were you I'd . . .' which makes the patient think (or even say), 'But you're *not* me.' Which really is a conversation-stopper.

10. *Encourage reminiscence.* Many patients – old and young – want to share reminiscences. Even children like to start stories about times when they were younger, and want to hear you re-tell the

events. For older patients, particularly if they happen to be your parents, reminiscences serve as reassurance that their lives have meaning. Sharing memories is often a bitter-sweet experience for them and for you. It may remind them of how much they're losing by dying and may make them cry; it may make you cry as well. If that happens, don't fight it. In practice, many psychotherapists and counsellors use it (the so-called 'guided autobiography') to encourage a patient to look at her past and tick what's right about it.

Another thing that may emerge from recovered memories is the way the patient has coped with previous setbacks – the loss of a job, a marital problem, a road accident. The way we cope with setbacks is part of our personality. Patients may think that they 'simply can't cope', but when they go back over the past they find that they have coped with all kinds of problems quite well. Sometimes, as a result of thinking about the past, the patient realises that she is actually quite good at coping and can use the same coping abilities now.

11. *Respond to humour.* Many people imagine that there cannot possibly be anything to laugh about if you are seriously ill or dying. However, they are missing an extremely important point about humour. Humour actually serves an important function in our way of coping with major threats and fears: it allows us to *ventilate*, to get rid of intense feelings and to get things in perspective. Humour is one of the ways in which human beings deal with things that seem impossible to deal with. If you think for a moment about the most common subjects of jokes, they include mothers-in-law, fear of flying, hospitals and doctors, sex, and so on. None of those things are intrinsically funny. An argument with a mother-in-law, for instance, can be very distressing for all concerned, not least for the daughter who is caught in a conflict of loyalties. But arguing with the mother-in-law has been an easy laugh for the stand-up comedian for centuries because we all laugh most easily at the things we cope with least easily. We laugh at things to get them in perspective, to reduce them in size and threat.

One patient I remember in particular was a woman in her early forties who had cancer of the cervix which eventually necessitated an in-dwelling catheter in her bladder. While she was in hospital she carried the drainage bag like a purse, and used to say loudly that it was a shame nobody made a drainage bag that matched her gloves. Out of context that may sound ghoulish or like 'gallows humour' but for this particular woman it was her personal method of dealing with a very distressing problem and demonstrated, I think, her true bravery and desire to rise above her physical problems. For her, it was very much in character.

From this experience and many others that I have shared with patients, I have become convinced that laughter helps the patient to get a different handle on his situation. This means that if *he* wants to use humour – even humour that to an outsider might seem like black humour – you should certainly encourage and go along with it, because it's helping him to cope. This does not mean that you should try to cheer him up with a supply of jokes – this simply doesn't work. You can best help your friend by responding sensitively. That means responding if you can to his humour, rather than trying to set the mood with your own.

I have one further comment on the subject of humour and illness. A number of people subscribe to the belief that laughter actually cures some physical illnesses. I remain very sceptical about this. It's a bit like other miracle-cure claims: there's no doubt that laughter makes you feel better. It raises the pain threshold among other things, and it may reduce the intensity of the symptoms. But I would need more convincing before I believed that it actually affected disease processes.

In summary, the objective of sensitive listening is to understand as completely as you can what the other person is feeling. You can never achieve complete understanding but the closer you get, the better the communication between you and your friend will be. You can even say that openly (for instance 'Try to help me to understand what you're feeling . . .') and *the more you try to understand your friend's feelings, the more support you are giving*.

3

Why You Need to Know What's Going On

Nothing in this book can, unfortunately, alter what is happening to your friend. But understanding what is going on can change its impact on you and on the relationship between you.

By comprehending what is happening and having some guidelines in your mind, you can change the way you respond. This happens in three ways:

1. *By your understanding and recognising what your friend is feeling and going through*. This will reduce the fear and panic that you feel, and will help you function normally in abnormal circumstances.

2. *By reacting differently yourself*. Once you identify the different emotions and feelings that your friend is experiencing, you can respond differently and may be able to turn, for instance, a potential argument into something that helps you both and brings you closer.

3. *By having some guidelines to work with*. Guidelines such as you will find in later chapters will stop you feeling overwhelmed and swept

away by events. The husband of a patient of mine told me how he felt when he and his wife first learned that her breast cancer had recurred in her spinal column: 'I felt absolutely paralysed. I had no idea what to do at all. I felt as if I just wanted to curl up in a ball and wish it all away. There were a hundred thoughts and a thousand questions going through my mind and I had absolutely no idea what to try and do first. So I felt as if I couldn't do anything – and that I'd never come out of that tailspin.'

By understanding the things that happen as someone becomes more ill and faces the threat of death, you will be able to reduce the sensation of paralysis and hang on to all of your normal thinking and planning resources.

These, then, are the three major ways in which understanding what is going on will help you. Before we move on to consider what happens in detail, I would like to use a simple example of how understanding the nature of an emotion can change your behaviour. Let us pick anger as a fairly common reaction with which everybody is familiar. We all have arguments among our family and friends and we all react quite naturally if someone is angry with us: we apologise, or get angry back, or ignore it (if we can). These are completely normal ways of reacting to somebody who's angry with us.

However, when somebody in your family or circle is facing a serious illness and death, the anger that they feel may really be directed at the illness; but it comes out directed at you because you are the only person around. If you are aware of the fact that the anger isn't *meant* for you personally, then you might be able to respond in a different way from the usual family-argument style. If you *are* able to respond differently, then you might allow the patient to defuse her anger and talk about it instead of simply boiling with it. Here's an example of what I mean:

Patient says something like:
'I feel dreadful and you're no help.'

↓

You have several choices:

If you react 'normally' (as in a family argument) you might say:	But if you realise that the anger is not directed at you personally, you might say:
↓	↓
'Well, I'm doing my best.' or *'Stop criticising me.'* or *'You're not easy to help.'*	*'How dreadful do you feel?'* or *'What's the most dreadful part?'* or *'You sound really low.'*
↓	↓
All these responses lead to escalation and a rift between you.	All of these responses encourage a dialogue and allow the patient to say more about what's on his mind.

If you're able to understand something of *why* the patient is saying what she's saying, then you may be able to respond in a way that eases her pain. That way, you become part of the solution; if you don't take time to understand what's going on, there's a danger you may become part of the problem.

PART TWO

The Transition

4
The Stages of Dying

Very few healthy people actually *want* to die, and very few seriously ill patients actually hasten their own deaths. We are all 'programmed' to hold on to life for as long as possible. This means that basically if somebody tells us we have an illness that may kill us we find it very difficult to accept it as a fact. Everybody facing the threat of death has to make a painful transition from thinking of themselves as perfectly healthy people (which is what we all do most of the time) to thinking of themselves as people who might die, and finally as people who *are going to* die. One can think of this transition as going from 'It won't happen to me (although I really know one day it might),' to 'It really might happen to me,' to 'It's happening to me.'

The transition consists of many stages, and it is difficult, no matter what age you are and what the nature of the illness is. In fact, I remember two patients who happened to be in adjacent rooms in one hospital a few years ago. Connie was in her mid-thirties and was very near the end of her life when I first met her. She and her husband had talked over every aspect of her dying, and had made all the arrangements for her to die at her home. She spoke sadly but lovingly of the beautiful view from her front room, and asked me to make sure that she was released from hospital as soon as possible so that she could spend her last few days looking at that view. She was an incredibly impressive woman, and her courage and calm struck a chord with everybody around her. She got her wish. In the next room was a woman called Barbara who was in her early seventies. Barbara was simply not ready to die; she was having great difficulty adjusting to her physical handicaps and even greater difficulty trying to sort out her family (she had two sons and a stepson who were bickering and arguing with each other). Barbara was very distressed by what was going on, and needed a lot of time and support. Only after several interviews did she begin to adjust her view of what was happening and become able to make many plans and arrangements that made things easier for her and her family.

The point is that for everyone going through this transition, no matter how old or young they are, there is a huge task of adjustment – and this is a time when a close friend or relative can be of real help.

To make it easier to understand what goes on during the transition, I've divided it up into three phases: a beginning phase, as the person faces the threat of death, an illness phase, as the person's pattern of living becomes altered by physical decline, and a final phase, as the person approaches death. Of course any division is artificial but in my experience as a doctor (and relative) I think these three phases are easy to understand and recognise, and a useful way to get a handle on a process which is continuous. In some respects, many continuous processes have similar features. Think of a trip or a journey, for instance: it may not be possible to say exactly when 'travelling' turns into 'nearly there', but nevertheless there are easily recognisable differences in the atmosphere between the mid-journey point and the nearly-there point. I am not claiming that there is anything unique in this division: – it is simply a description that I have found most useful and practical.

However, on the subject of transition, I need to make a point about other people's thinking. Many people have written about dying, and the most renowned of these authors is Dr Elisabeth Kübler-Ross. I mention her work because many readers may know about it and wonder if I am striking out on my own or trying to disprove her views. In fact, I differ only in some minor respects.

Dr Kübler-Ross divided the process of dying into five stages: denial, anger, bargaining, depression and acceptance. In doing this I think that she highlighted five extremely important aspects of dying, but in my view she has described types of *reactions* and not stages. I find that there are many kinds of reaction other than those five, including fear, anxiety, hope and guilt. In this section of the book I shall illustrate the various reactions and shall show you that some kinds of reaction are more common near the beginning, some are more common during the illness and some are more common at the end. Many people are, for example, angry and depressed (at the same time) at the beginning and become more accepting near the end. Rather than follow the Kübler-Ross scheme, therefore, I am going to discuss the most common kinds of reaction in each of the three phases as I see them. There is no right and wrong about this. We are all simply looking for useful ways of describing this important transition in a way that is easy to understand. If you find that my description makes the process intelligible and gives you some guidelines to helping your friend through the various phases, then I shall have done what I set out to do.

However, before going on to the details of these reactions, there are a few general points that need underlining. First of all, each one of us is capable of feeling several emotions at the same time (this may sound obvious but it's easy to forget). Think what happens when a child gets separated from a parent in a shop or a crowd. When they find each other the parent is usually immensely relieved and pleased, but also angry with the child for getting lost. She may also feel an additional tinge of guilt for having lost concentration for a moment. Now if I were describing such a scene to you, I would mention the relief and the anger separately – even though they crop up simultaneously. And that's what I'm doing in this book. I know I'm describing a mixture or a salad of emotions, but I can only do it one ingredient at a time. It's important not to forget that *all human beings are capable of experiencing several different emotions at the same time*.

Second, even though I'm going to describe the transition in three phases, these aren't hard-and-fast rules that the patient *has* to stick to. Some people may react with only one or two patterns, others may show many. And, far more important, people facing death often go forwards and backwards in their understanding of what's going on. In other words, things tend to change from day to day. A patient may reach acceptance of his situation on Monday and show denial or anger on Tuesday. It's no help for the friend to get annoyed and say something like, 'Hey, wait a minute, you understood it all yesterday, you're not supposed to be angry again today.' Nor does it mean that you, as the friend, have got it wrong or misunderstood the situation – you just have to be aware that human emotions change constantly, like waves and eddies on a beach, even while there is an easily recognisable major change going on as the tide comes in. Even the tidiest and conceptually neatest ways of considering this process have their limitations – no one goes through the process of dying in a regimented way according to some textbook, even if it's written by an expert.

It's particularly important that you understand the lack of order and predictability, precisely because the patterns are so variable and individual. Some people are already physically very ill at the time of first diagnosis. They may even be near death. Others may feel completely well physically at the time of diagnosis and have great difficulty in understanding that they have a lethal condition even while they feel well. Similarly, some people will adjust to the ending of their lives relatively early in the course of the disease (whether they are young or old), and others will not allow themselves to recognise the imminence of death at all. As long as you know that there is this wide variation among people, then you won't be put off by it, and will still be able to help your friend as he experiences different emotions.

The last general point I want to make is this: in most illnesses there is a measure of uncertainty, and sometimes there seems to be nothing but uncertainty. Will the pain be relieved? How long will the patient live? Is there any hope at all? Now, to many of these crucial questions there may be no answer. It may not be possible for doctors (or anyone else) to tell how long the patient may live or what the future will be like. Most people find that living with that kind of uncertainty is awful – which it undoubtedly is. You need to know that, so that you realise that it's very likely to hurt, and that if it does hurt you're not being abnormal. *Living with uncertainty is painful in itself.*

5

Facing the Threat

Whether your friend is feeling physically well or extremely ill when the diagnosis is made, there is still a moment at which he comes up against the threat of the end of life, not as an idea or something that happens to other people, but as a probability or certainty. The vast mental adjustments that all of us, as human beings, have to undergo are the subject of this chapter.

Human minds are not very good at coping with bad news in the abstract. When we hear news that may drastically affect our future, we find it difficult to 'get a fix on it'. This is the way human minds are organised and it means that the person hearing bad news has to struggle with it. Several different kinds of reaction may emerge from this struggle. Some of these reactions may seem at first peculiar. They may make us (as supporters and observers) want to say to the patient something like, 'Why are you behaving like this? — This *isn't you*.' But it *is* him or her — it's just that facing a new threat is *so* unusual that what you, as the friend or relative, are seeing is the normal behaviour of the patient in a new and abnormal situation.

Even if, at this moment, you're caring for someone who was told her diagnosis some time ago, perhaps even years ago, I hope you'll continue to read this section. Reactions that begin at the time of diagnosis continue throughout the whole illness, and even in retrospect may shed some light on what's going on for you now.

The Patient's Feelings

Shock and disbelief

Most of us use words like 'shock' and 'disbelief' over trivial things. We are simply indicating that events are a little unusual ('It always rains the day I get the windows cleaned – I don't believe it.') When an event is so far out of the range of normal day-to-day living that the patient really *does* have serious difficulty in taking the news on board, it's often difficult for her to find the right words to express it.

Almost every patient facing the threat of terminal illness and death goes through some phase of shock and disbelief, whether it is a short phase measured in hours or days, or a phase so long that she never seems to emerge from it completely.

In practice, true disbelief is that stage in which the patient cannot incorporate the news into her view of the world, although she may be able to think and behave normally intermittently. Almost always, the believing of bad news comes and goes in the early stages. The patient may be able to accept it and get to grips with it one evening, and wake the next morning wondering whether it is real after all. Patients often say things like 'I keep on thinking it's all a dream.' This is the expression of genuine disbelief and it is a completely normal reaction to overwhelming news.

Shock, on the other hand, in the ordinary use of the word, implies a bigger impact on the patient's ability to think and behave. Shock means the stopping of normal thoughts and emotions. It is more like a *degree* of reaction, or an indication of the *severity* of a reaction, than a different *kind* of reaction in itself. Shock, like disbelief, waxes and wanes.

The most common symptom of shock is a breakdown in the ability to make decisions. Of course we all experience some diffi- culty in making decisions at various stressful points in our lives, but in a state of shock even relatively simple decisions seem impossible and cannot be made. Other symptoms include forgetfulness – not remembering familiar phone numbers and names. The person in shock may also simply slow down: simple actions like getting dressed or cooking meals take a very long time; she may go shopping and forget why she's there. She may often seem to be staring into space and lost to the outside world for a time. Often, while the person in this state seems on the surface to be inert and apathetic, there is a cauldron of emotions mixing and bubbling inside her. There may also be a great deal of clinging and a loss of independence – a desire to be looked after in what may at first seem a very childlike way. This, then, is the typical picture of a patient in shock.

For the patient it is a highly unpleasant and distressing state to be in. It is often made worse because the patient *realises* that he is in a mess, and may feel that he should be able simply to snap out of it. It is very important for you to know that no one *can* snap out of it, but that this shocked and non-functioning phase is truly a phase, and a normal but severe reaction to overwhelming news. Most people do not recover instantly, or by simply 'pulling themselves together', but usually recover gradually over a period of time.

As time goes on, then, the sensation of being shocked should fade. There will be no fixed schedule, but if the shocked state really doesn't fade, and the patient seems unable to function normally and shows no signs of getting any normal functions back, even for short periods, you may need to get some expert help for the patient. It is worth discussing this with the patient's doctor.

Denial

There is a real difference between 'denial' and 'disbelief'. Disbelief can be summarised as 'I can't take this on board (even though I'm trying),' whereas denial is 'I'm not going to take this on board (even though I could).' Denial can happen at several levels. It can be completely involuntary or it can be partly voluntary. Sometimes it's involuntary in the sense that the patient might *appear* to be trying to come to terms with the situation, but at a deeper level may have blocked off, and subconsciously 'decided' not to come to terms.

Denial can occur even if the person is very well informed. It does not indicate that the patient is unintelligent or losing his mind. A very well-known physician was admitted to his own hospital for an exploratory operation. It showed that he had advanced cancer of the pancreas which was, in his case, incurable. He was told the diagnosis by the surgeon a few days after the operation, but every day after that he asked the surgeon the same question, 'What did the operation show?' The surgeon (who knew the patient well as a colleague and as a friend) answered each day, 'It showed cancer of the pancreas – we told you yesterday.' To which the patient would always answer, 'Oh yes, of course – you told me yesterday,' but would ask the same question the following day. It was nearly two weeks before the patient found that he could remember being told the diagnosis.

Another doctor, a family practitioner who developed cancer of the prostate, expressed it perfectly when he told me about the way he felt after the operation at which the diagnosis was made. He said, 'It wasn't as if I couldn't believe the diagnosis; I was just absolutely *certain* in my heart that it wasn't cancer. I assumed there was a mix-up with the laboratory results. Actually I didn't just *think* there was a mistake, I was absolutely *sure* of it. I even telephoned the pathologist and when he told me it was cancer of the prostate I just thought he'd made the same mistake as everyone else. I knew all about the process of denial in other people – I'd seen it many times with my patients when I had to tell them bad news, and I was always quite good at helping them through it. But while all this was going on with me I was sure that this wasn't a case of denial at work. I just kept on thinking, "This isn't prostate cancer. It isn't happening to me – it's not my turn yet". The feelings only began to fade after three weeks, nearly a month.'

The important point is that denial is a *conflict* between knowledge and belief. While the patient's mind telling him that what is happening *is* real, the emotion of denial can be so powerful (even if that mind is crammed with medical facts and information) that the person simply cannot believe the facts that his mind feeding him.

As someone close to the patient, you should be aware of the power of the denial reaction. If you underestimate that power you might think your friend is being 'silly' or even losing his mind. This is not the case. Denial is a normal coping mechanism of the human mind. It will usually fade away in time, allowing the patient to accept the bad news without being swamped by it.

You also need to be aware of the power of denial because you cannot wipe it out by simply *confronting* the patient with the facts. Although that approach might seem sensible ('I'll just tell him what's really going on'), in practice it does not achieve anything. You merely appear as an adversary to the patient or part of the conspiracy against him. I shall illustrate some methods of dealing with denial at the end of this chapter, but for now let me stress that there *are* ways in which you can leave the door open for further discussion about the facts, without actually confronting the patient and thrusting the facts down his throat.

Sometimes, then, denial can be a powerful and involuntary reaction to threatening news. On other occasions it can be quite plain and direct – several patients have given me fairly clear guidelines on what they will or will not listen to. Several times, I've been given a clear instruction on the lines of: 'Don't tell me any bad news, Doctor – if it's serious, talk to my wife.'

In those circumstances, the underlying emotion that the person is feeling is probably something like this: 'I know deep down how bad the news is, but just at the moment I don't want to face it in the open.' This may be a perfectly acceptable and useful way for the person to cope with the news, either temporarily or even permanently, if there is no pressing need for the patient to know precisely what's going on. But this raises a most important issue – does the patient *need* to know what's going on? In other words, does denial matter and is it necessary for the patient to face up to the bald facts? In some ways this is the most important question to be answered when it comes to facing bad news, and it's worth looking at it from several different viewpoints.

Should the patient be told?

Some doctors specialising in the care of the dying maintain that the task of facing up to the news is absolutely essential, and that you simply cannot approach the end of your life properly unless you face it directly and come to accept it. On the other hand, many families of patients feel the exact opposite: they think that if the patient knows how bad things are the knowledge itself will hasten the end of their life and rob them of their will to live. They say, 'Don't tell our mother she's got cancer, Doctor. The news alone would kill her.'

Thus some people support the view that *any* form of denial is wrong, while others think the opposite, that sharing information is dangerous and that denial should be *inflicted* on the patient whatever her real wishes are. It is worth considering these issues in detail.

Let us start with the idea that patients shouldn't be told bad news at all. This is not a helpful way to treat someone. Several studies of patients in cancer wards show that the majority of patients really do want to know exactly what's going on, and *need* to know in order to make intelligent plans. Furthermore, studies comparing the mental state of patients who do *not* know what is going on, compared with those who do, show that patients who are kept in the dark have far greater problems with depression, anxiety and a sense of isolation. In my own practice I have listened to many patients who have told me specifically how bad they felt when they were not told what was going on. I have heard many descriptions of these feelings of isolation, mistrust and, sometimes, desperation. Most of these feelings faded away when the patient was given the information he wanted.

One patient put it into words very neatly. He was an intelligent businessman in his early thirties who for six years had had occasional symptoms of unsteadiness when walking, and pins and needles around his face. In fact, he had early (and fairly mild) multiple sclerosis, but two successive doctors whom he had consulted had refused to tell him what was wrong. He told me in a television interview what it was like not being told what was wrong with him. He said it was just like going to his bank, asking for the balance of his account, and being told 'It isn't anything to worry about,' and that he should 'Go home and not think about it.' When he was told the diagnosis by a third doctor a few years later he felt a sense of relief, and felt, for the first time, that he was being treated as a human being and an equal. He felt that his previous doctors had insulted him and patronised him by withholding information that was so important to him.

I would add that, if we feel angry and insulted when we are not told something as simple as our bank balance, we are likely to feel much more insulted if it is something of far greater significance such as the state of our health and our future.

Some people genuinely do not want to know what is going on in detail, and do not want the facts explained to them, but there is strong evidence to show that most people do want to know. Several studies have been done by psychiatrists of patients with newly diagnosed cancers in order to find out how many patients really do want to know. These studies show that at least 50 per cent, and perhaps as many as 80 per cent, would like to know what's going on. In other words if you (whether you are a doctor or a relative) think that nobody should be told what's going on, you will be wrong at least half the time, and possibly three-quarters of the time.

Gradually, the medical profession is accepting this information. Nowadays, the kind of doctor who *never* tells the patient the facts is becoming something of a rarity.

It is therefore crucial that if a patient *wants* to know what is going on he or she must be told. To do anything else is unfair and unjust. Not only that, but to withhold information may be infringing the patient's rights – ethical, moral, and in some countries legal. It is rapidly being accepted by the medical profession (prompted by the legal case precedence, particularly in the United States) that a patient has a *right* to information that concerns him or her, and that the decision whether to exercise that right or not is the patient's and nobody else's. Things are still in a state of change in Britain as regards the law on this point, but in the United States and similarly in Canada the rights of the patient are being defined ever more clearly in ethical and legal terms.

What if the patient doesn't want to know?
If it appears that the patient does not want to know, there are two criteria by which you can assess the situation. First, is there any particular *need* for the patient to know; and second, is the patient becoming *distressed* by not knowing?

There may be several needs that simply cannot be addressed unless the patient is fully in the picture. There may be medical needs, such as treatment choices and options, which cannot be offered unless the patient understands the nature and gravity of the disease. This is often the case with cancer treatments, which usually cannot be given unless the patient is aware of the need for them and of the side-effects.

I have a very vivid memory of a patient with cancer of the ovary whom I first met several years ago. The letter from her doctor said, 'She will simply not allow me to tell her what is going on, and I am concerned that you may not be able to offer her treatment.' She was an exceptionally nervous woman and her first words to me were, 'If it's cancer, I don't want you to tell me.' I assured her that I would not and asked about her fears of cancer. She told me of the deaths of five members of her family years ago, and the sufferings that they had endured. Her main fears were of similar suffering. She thought that if she *knew* it was cancer all the fight would go out of her. We talked for about half an hour and I described the treatment in detail and mentioned the various support services that we could offer (including more conversations about her fears). When she heard about the treatment she recognised it as chemotherapy and, when I said it was, she smiled broadly (for the first time) and said, 'Oh well, I knew it was cancer anyway.' From that moment on, she relaxed and was able to tolerate the treatment and several ups and downs of her disease with considerable calm.

This example illustrates one of the circumstances in which the medical needs of a patient dictate the sharing of part of the information. It shows that patients who may appear 'not to want to know' may know very well what is going on, but need a supportive atmosphere to share their fears. It also shows that you do not have to force a confrontation to deal with the apparent denial. Usually this type of situation is of greater importance in the relationship between the patient and doctor, so it is perhaps somewhat beyond the scope of this book, but still important for you as friend and supporter to know about.

Apart from concerns about medical treatment, there may be other reasons for a patient's need to know what is going on. These include plans for the future that may involve the patient, friends and family. Plans may be needed for business, buying or selling homes, arranging trips and holidays and so on. Most of us make decisions about things like that all the time, on the subconscious assumption that we are going to live for a long time, or at least long enough to see the completion of the plans. If, however, we had a serious illness, we might well make different plans. It is therefore very important for supporters and friends of the patient to think about whether the patient is making plans that would be altered by the news. Is he saving up for a cruise or a special event far into the future? Is he just about to enter a big business venture that depends on his personal abilities and would be jeopardised if he were seriously ill or dying? If so, then you will need to explore the sharing of the news further (and I shall be explaining more about how to do this later on).

Let us suppose that the patient has no medical reasons and no important family reasons for needing to know about the future. What then? Is denial 'all right' in these circumstances, or should the facts be thrust upon the patient until they are accepted fully? The single most important consideration here is the distress of the patient. If the person is completely calm and tranquil and able to communicate freely and function normally *without* knowing what's going on, then this should be accepted by friends and family (and doctors) and the facts should not be thrust upon the patient.

If, on the other hand, the patient is apparently saying 'I don't want to know, don't tell me,' but is, in the process, suffering much distress, then often the situation can be improved by probing and by sharing the facts. Quite often the patient really *wants* to ask the questions but feels that he or she is not *brave* enough to cope with the answer. This is an exceptionally difficult area to cope with, and you will need help from any sympathetic and skilled helpers (whether they are doctors, nurses, social workers, clergy or psychologists) if you find yourself supporting a patient in this state.

The most difficult example of this that I can recall was a young woman called Annie. She was twenty-three years old and dying of a rare cancer that had proved resistant to all forms of therapy. When I first met her she was paralysed from the mid-chest region downwards, had difficulty in breathing (because of secondary tumours in her lungs) and was in moderate-to-severe pain as a result of other tumours pressing on several nerves. She was extremely bright and intelligent and had obviously been (before the changes resulting from the illness and the treatment) an attractive woman. At our first meeting, it seemed to me that she was absolutely determined not to acknowledge to me or anyone else how serious her condition was. Her sister (who was herself a doctor) told me that Annie was in great pain at home and needed high doses of pain-killers, but put on a brave front for her visits to the hospital (including taking a great deal of trouble over her make-up). I wanted to improve control of the pain, but Annie simply said (several times) that everything was fine and that she experienced only a little pain now and then. She also denied that she was short of breath even though she could hardly finish a whole sentence.

During our conversation she seemed, almost literally, to be gritting her teeth and holding back any indication that things weren't going well. Her mother and father, to whom she was very close, were deeply distressed both by Annie's physical condition and by the way she wouldn't let anybody 'in' to help her.

It was clear to me that Annie was keen not to let the side down, and not to be seen as someone who had failed her medical team when they had done their best for her. Near the end of our second conversation she mentioned a dream that she'd had about a friend of hers, Jenny, who had tragically committed suicide a few years previously. In the dream, Annie and Jenny were on a bus together and Jenny would not allow Annie to get off at her home, but told her that she was to stay on the bus to the end of the journey. This was the only indication that Annie had even thought about dying. I asked her if she had any religious convictions and, if so, whether she would agree to see our clinic chaplain, John Martin.

John had two interviews with Annie that accomplished a great deal in a relatively short time. Annie spoke of her last conversation with Jenny before the suicide; Jenny had not said anything to

Annie that indicated she was contemplating suicide. Annie spoke to John about the rage that she, Annie, had felt at Jenny's death, and still felt. She said, 'If only she'd told me what she was feeling, we could have talked about so much.' John replied, 'Does that sound familiar?' This made Annie suddenly realise how much she herself was holding back from her family, and how that must be making *them* feel angry and distressed just as she had felt about Jenny. For the first time in the hospital, Annie cried and spoke at length about how she was trying to protect her family from what was happening by not talking to them. John showed her that by doing this she was excluding her family and hurting them. He explained to her that her feelings were normal and not shameful or a sign of weakness.

At the end of the interview Annie acknowledged openly a lot of the fear and the pain that she was feeling. She admitted that perhaps it wasn't such a good idea to use so much effort to keep up a front and hide her feelings. She said to John, 'Thank you for giving me the courage not to be courageous.' We later heard that in the next few days she was able to tell her parents how much she loved them and how she wanted to be able to say goodbye to them but found it difficult; and she was also able to communicate more freely with her sister. She died a few weeks later.

The point of recounting those events is to show that sometimes denial is very damaging to both the family and the patient, and that you, as friends and care-givers, may need to call in some expert and willing help precisely because the immediate helpers are being excluded, as Annie's family and I were. It may well be that the chaplain or minister is in the best position to help, but if your friend doesn't happen to have strong religious convictions, then other helpers such as social workers, psychologists or nurses may be able to achieve this. This kind of denial is hard on the patient, hard on you and hard on anyone who has to look after the patient.

In summary, information should always be offered, but sometimes it is rejected. If there is no medical or social need to deal with that information, then I think that you, as the friend of the patient, can be comfortable in leaving the denial alone and accepting it as the way in which this particular person is dealing with the threat. If, on the other hand, there are reasons that the patient *has* to know what's going on, or if the denial is causing great distress to the patient, then you should look for some expert help.

There are some practical tips on this subject in the third section of this chapter, 'A guide to giving support'.

Anger

Anger at some stage of a serious illness is very common. It is actually common in any illness, whether serious or trivial, but with simple and self-limiting illnesses – flu for example – the anger fades as the patient recovers, whereas with chronic illness the anger is there every day.

Why do we get angry when we're ill? The single most important reason is loss of control. Most of us try hard to have control over most of the things that happen in our lives – at all stages and all the time. We do things that involve personal choices and decisions – and we expect, and often get, the freedom to make those choices. Whether it's taking a decision personally at work, or deciding whether to overtake on the motorway, we spend a lot of our time proving our control over events by making our own decisions. Generally speaking, we don't like it when we have no say in events. Much of the rage and unhappiness, for instance, that is caused when a factory is closed down is due to the feeling of powerlessness experienced by the people thrown out of work. Of course not everyone is like this. A few people genuinely enjoy living with decisions and choices made by other people or made at random, but, by and large, most of us would prefer things to happen our way.

The problem is that illness *doesn't* happen our way. It happens its own way. And in exactly the same way in which factory workers resent the powerlessness that is forced on them by a closure, so someone who is ill often resents the loss of control over his own body and his own fate.

There are several kinds of anger that people experience, and they can be divided into three major types:

1. *Anger at the rest of the world*, including friends and relatives and everybody who isn't ill, all of whom are going to carry on living. (The 'why me?' anger).

2. *Anger directed at any recognisable form of fate*, or destiny or controlling influence that has allowed this to happen (in people who have religious beliefs this anger may be directed at God, or may cause a loss of religious faith).

3. *Anger at anyone who is trying to help*, particularly doctors and nurses (the 'blaming-the-bearer-for-the-bad-news' reaction).

Anger at everyone who is healthy is an extremely common

emotion. The words 'why me?' crop up so often in television plays and films that the phrase may seem to be no more than a cliché. In reality, it is a very genuine and deeply felt emotion; although 'why me?' can sometimes sound like a question it is usually a cry of anger, often with frustration and sometimes desperation added.

As a relative or someone close to the patient, you might easily be the target of that anger. It may not seem fair that you, in trying to do your best to help, should be the first in the firing line, but it happens quite often and is certainly not abnormal or a sign of something fundamentally wrong in the relationship between you and your friend. The most important point to remember is that you should respond to 'why me?' as you would to a cry of pain (or of despair), rather than by trying to *answer* it as a question. I shall illustrate various ways of responding to 'why me?' at the end of this chapter.

The second kind of anger – directed against fate or God – is also common and very real. I shall deal with that in greater detail in Chapter 9 but perhaps should just note that this kind of anger raises very fundamental questions about the way the patient sees the whole world, so it is not the kind of reaction that can be passed off with a consoling phrase.

The third kind of anger is specifically directed at the people who are trying to help and it is also quite common and complex. Although it is perhaps less directly relevant to friends and family, this kind of anger can drastically affect the relationship between the patient and the doctor – which may rebound on you in several ways, making it difficult for you to help the patient. For instance you may be asked to take sides and judge between patient and doctor. Or because of your involvement with the patient you may find yourself pitched against the doctor. (I am not, of course, implying that doctors never deserve to be blamed, but on many occasions the blame is really directed against the disease, not the doctor). For these reasons, then, it is worth considering this particular kind of anger a little further.

Doctors are blamed for the illness itself because the transaction between doctor and patient superficially resembles many other normal transactions of daily life. Society and the medical profession have endowed a consultation with a doctor with the same sort of expectations as, say, a visit to the garage. Many patients hope and perhaps expect that the doctor will explain what is going wrong, and that he or she will repair the defect in the same way as a car mechanic repairs a car. But there are many important differences between medical and mechanical problems, of which the most important is that in medicine there are no guarantees. So, if you are accustomed to getting a guarantee from your car mechanic and if you are accustomed to complaining if he does not deliver what is promised, you will be primed to expect the same of your doctor. If, later, the disease turns out to be incurable you will have a tendency to be angry because your expectations have not been met. The more modern medicine comes to resemble a business, the more patients expect the rights of a paying customer, and the more difficult it becomes to accept that many diseases are simply not fixable.

This underscores the reasons why patients become angry when they are dealing with a disease and why they commonly, at some stage in the illness, blame the doctor for the illness. You may become involved in this kind of a reaction as a bystander called in to adjudicate, or you may become the target yourself. You need to be aware (yet again) that this is a common form of reaction to serious illness, and although it may *seem* to be directed at you in a very personal way, it isn't really meant personally.

Fear

Fear of serious illness and death are so common, in our society at least, that we would normally regard someone who was not frightened as crazy. Fear of dying is at the core of this book, and if fear of dying was something with which we could all cope, this book would be unnecessary. But there are several features that are commonly overlooked in thinking about fears in general, and about fear of dying in particular.

Not only is fear very common, but also most of us are brought up to be *afraid of being afraid* – or, at least, to be ashamed of being afraid. In a way, most of us have an idea at the back of our minds that we're not *supposed* to be afraid of things. Of course, almost everybody is afraid of something. Even the people who strenuously deny that they're afraid of anything may be afraid of admitting that they have one or two fears, for instance.

Two points need emphasising:

First, to be afraid you have to have imagination. If you have no imagination whatsoever (a rare phenomenon) and cannot imagine any of the possible consequences of what's going on, then you will not be frightened. There is insufficient space in this book for a detailed discussion of all the ingredients that make up a fear, but it is important to realise that people are afraid because they are *thinking* and they are *imagining*. It is one disadvantage of having an active and functioning mind; it is certainly not a sign of stupidity or 'low moral fibre'.

Second, fear of dying is not one fear but many fears. Every person has a different list of fears about illness and death – a little like a personal agenda or menu, perhaps. There are many different elements and combinations.

There are fears to do with physical illness and incapacity: fears of being handicapped, of being a burden on friends and family, and fears of being unable to contribute to family life.

There are fears about physical pain: how much suffering will there be and how will I stand up to it? What if I can't cope, and show that I'm a coward? What happens if my family see aspects of me that I've always managed to hide from them so far?

Then there are fears that are sometimes called 'existential' fears about the ending of life itself, the end of existence. And spiritual fears: What happens afterwards? Will there simply be oblivion? Will there be an afterlife and could there be punishment?

There are fears to do with the achievements of the person's life, fear of dying while some of life's potential is unfulfilled, fear of not having achieved enough, of not having succeeded and of not having made the best use of time. There may also be fears and concerns to do with rifts between family and friends, fences that should have been mended some time ago and that now may seem to be irreparable.

And there are practical fears of what may happen to the children or to the surviving spouse, to the business, to the running of the home, and so on.

We shall consider how these fears can be aired in the later part of this chapter, but for now I want to emphasise the fact that each individual has his or her own list of fears of illness and death – and that you, as supporter and friend, cannot know what is on that list unless you ask. If you help the person to talk about what is on that list, you will be giving an enormous amount of help. If you've never done anything like it before, you may think that it is like opening a Pandora's box or a pressure-cooker, and that you will be overwhelmed by what emerges. This doesn't happen. In the vast majority of instances, you will bring relief by assisting the patient to talk about his pent-up fears. All you need to do is to allow the patient the time and space to ventilate what's on his mind, and to stay close while he does so. In almost every instance this will make things better than they were while the patient was left to stew in his own mounting fear.

Hope, despair and depression

Facing up to the possibility (or probability) of the end of life is a monumental task for the patient. It seems to be the worst thing that could possibly happen, and that once the hope of a longer healthy life has gone, there is nothing left but despair.

Despair, like anger, fear and denial, is a very common phase in facing the threat of dying. There is no magic formula that will instantly banish it. The word 'despair' really means the loss of hope. The way we think of the word in daily use suggests that it is the opposite of hope, and that the only 'cure' for despair is hope. The problem is that there are many different kinds of hope, and some hopes (particularly false hopes about the outcome of the illness) can actually be *un*helpful to the patient.

Usually despair comes and goes in cycles. Like shock, despair is an emotion that tends to overwhelm the patient for a time, then partially fade and then return and so on. No one knows precisely why that is. I have postulated that it is because the human mind is an adaptive system that does not function very well under extremes of emotion. Hence, in my view, our minds are pro-grammed to try to level off and return to a 'normal state' as soon as possible after a large emotional shock. Very often this adaptive mechanism works. This is how people are able to do normal things like cooking very soon after major shocks such as floods or earthquakes: it is a survival mechanism built into the way our minds work.

What we often see, then, in patients facing terminal illness is despair that comes in waves, and very often when the despair ebbs away and fades the patient overswings into one or more hopes. This cycle is a very common way of adapting to the bad news, and in most cases what happens is that the depth of the 'lows' and the height of the 'highs' decrease so that the swings become less violent and extreme. This is the normal adapting process, and you need to be aware of it because you need to realise that if your friend is in despair on Tuesday and feeling optimistic on Wednesday, it doesn't mean he won't be feeling low again on Thursday. And if he *does* feel low on Thursday it doesn't mean he's mad, or losing his mind, or manic depressive.

You also need to be aware of this because you have to realise that despair can never be cured by false hope. The trouble is that friends (and doctors and nurses, too) are often tempted to try injecting hope, often encouraged by the patient. That's because it feels very uncomfortable to be near someone who is in deep despair. We feel their pain and we'd like to relieve it. The trouble is that if you try to inject false hope all that happens is that you relieve the pain for a moment or so but create worse pain later on when the hopes are not fulfilled.

I'd like to say a word or two about the two words 'depression' and 'despair'. Depression refers to a lowness of mood and spirits and it is quite possible to be depressed without being in despair. Despair has something to do with absence of hope and therefore has a lot to do with the dying person's outlook. In practical terms, despair is almost always accompanied by depression, but not everyone who is depressed is in despair. However, these distinctions are not of major practical importance. For a start, both despair and depression come and go in cycles, and second what really matters is how bad they are.

Medically, we recognise certain physical signs of depression including inability to sleep (usually waking in the small hours and being unable to get back to sleep), crying much of the time, loss of appetite and loss of interest in conversation and interactions with other people, loss of facial expression, and particularly loss of smiling. Now I don't want to turn you into a doctor, all I want to do is alert you to the signals of major depression, because severe and prolonged depression can be helped by medication, and if you are aware of the depth of your friend's depression you can call it to the attention of the doctor looking after her. Of course symptoms such as loss of appetite or sleep may be due to other causes, such as the disease itself, or uncontrolled pain. It is a matter for the doctor to decide whether the patient is going through major depression that will be helped by antidepressants, or whether it is a deep sadness that is part of the adjustment process. Doctors' opinions may vary, but you can help best by checking that the doctor is aware of the depth of the problem. Many patients put on a brave face for the doctor and only reveal the genuine agony to relatives and friends. As a doctor it's happened many times that I have found out the real situation only from discussions with the supporting members of family or circle.

The medical team may well call in a psychiatrist to help your friend cope with severe depression. It needs to be said clearly and often that needing the help of a psychiatrist doesn't mean the patient is mad or losing his or her mind. It's simply that the assessment of the depth of depression, judging how the patient is coping, and what kind of help is required, is a job for people who are experts in that field – and that usually means psychiatrists. It sounds as if it might be quite easy to judge how deeply depressed someone is, but often it's not: distinguishing severe depression from a transient sadness requires skill and experience. I spend a lot of my time looking after seriously ill and dying patients, and I still find quite regularly that I need to call in a psychiatrist to help me assess the way someone is reacting, and to help me to help them. Often the patient's first reaction when I mention that I am thinking of asking a psychiatrist's opinion is something like, 'First I get an illness, then I find I'm going to die, now you think I'm losing my mind as well.' Well, it really isn't like that. With the many different kinds of therapy that are available (and different medications including anti-depressants) you need experts – including psychiatrists – to decide which will be the most appropriate form of help.

Before we finish looking at the various aspects of loss of hope, we ought to consider for a moment the hopes of miracles and miracle cures that are commonly raised by friends and family of patients. There is no doubt that there are many people who are alive and well today who were told by their doctors that they were going to die years or months ago, and their example is often cited to bring hope to others. It is absolutely true that doctors are not brilliant at predicting survival of individual people, and that when they do make a prediction they are very often wrong. (I regularly have to say that the only thing I'm certain of is my own uncertainty in matters like this.) However, if there are people, however few, who have survived, apparently miraculously, then how can someone close to the patient deny them hope? Why shouldn't we spend all our time and energy hoping or praying for a miracle, and travelling to any place that we can afford where a miracle might be obtained for the patient?

These are difficult questions, to which there are no simple answers, but there are ways of dealing with despair and with desperate hopes of miracles, and we'll come back to them in Chapter 7. The point I'd like to make here is that human beings are often quite good at planning for the worst while hoping for the best. In other words, if you help your friend the patient to make plans for the worst, and something miraculous *does* occur, then the only thing you've done is waste time and effort on unnecessary arrangements. If, on the other hand, you spend all your time together hoping that the disease will go away and it does *not* resolve, then the patient will be unprepared and overwhelmed by events.

Finally, I should like to discuss bargaining. Bargaining is a reaction the patient may express in many ways. It may be a transaction between patient and doctor: 'If I agree to have the treatment, will you promise me it will work?' It may often be a private pact made by the patient with himself in which the patient promises that he will change some aspect of behaviour (such as smoking, being bad-tempered, not spending enough time at home) as an offering to propitiate the disease and to make it go away. It may also be a pact between the patient and his God: 'Get me out of this and I'll go to church every Sunday'.

Bargaining is a battle between hope and despair. In a bargaining process the patient says, 'I partly accept that the disease is upon me, but I am only prepared to accept it if I can make it go away, and here is what I am prepared to do to make it go away.' Bargaining, then, like denial, is one mechanism by which the human mind adjusts to the threat of dying and accepts it in small pieces rather than being overwhelmed by it. Bargaining is not a stage of the dying process, but is the result of the struggle within the patient's mind between the reality of the situation and the forces of hope and despair.

In summary, coping with despair is one of the most difficult aspects of supporting a dying person and it is often this aspect that takes the greatest toll from the friend in terms of effort and, sometimes, exhaustion. Later in this chapter I shall suggest some practical ways of approaching this very tough problem.

Guilt

When anyone becomes seriously ill, guilt seems to accumulate everywhere. It seems to fall out of the sky like a sudden shower, and it can be most destructive. It is not easy to define guilt in simple terms, but the most consistent feature is the feeling of responsibility, whether or not it is justified. If my daughter falls into a swimming-pool fully clothed (which she once did), I might feel guilty (which I did), and that guilt might be justified (which it was).

If, however, my daughter becomes ill, I might easily feel just as guilty even though I am not responsible at all. At the centre of any discussion about guilt, then, are two concepts: the whole idea of personal *responsibility*, and the normal consequence of being held responsible, punishment.

Guilt is such a common emotion because our society has deeply ingrained ideas of reward and punishment, and of responsibility. Everyone tends to feel guilty when there is a catastrophe (such as a serious illness) because our society is organised to expect that for every catastrophe there must be someone to blame. There is considerable cultural variation within different societies, but basically every culture has strong lines of responsibility running through its traditions which are reflected in its laws. Think for a moment about the massive investigations that take place if there is an air crash or an accident at a factory or a mine. The purpose of those investigations is to establish what happened, who is responsible and to whom sufferers or their families can apply for compensation. This process is so much a part of our social system that most of us would never think about it consciously but accept it as an absolute fact of life. Every society has some system of reward and punishment, from the earliest aboriginal cultures to apparently lawless groups such as Hell's Angels. These codes of reward and punishment are, in large part, what holds the particular group together and gives the members of the group identity as part of that group.

Of course there are natural disasters (earthquakes, storms and so on) for which no blame can be apportioned to a specific person or company – but isn't it interesting that insurance companies call these events 'acts of God', which is a way of fixing the blame elsewhere instead of acknowledging that there is no blame at all? However, these natural disasters apart, we all tend to grow up thinking, 'If something bad has happened, it must be somebody's fault,' and it therefore follows that in moments of calamity we are, in a way, brought up to look around for the cause of that calamity.

The threat of death is certainly widely regarded as a calamity, so we all have a strong tendency to allocate the blame for it. The first consequence of this is that the patient himself may regard the illness as a *punishment for sins committed in the past*.

To make matters worse, there are some diseases that we know *are* caused by personal habits: cirrhosis of the liver can be caused by alcohol abuse, for example, and cancer of the lung is caused by smoking. These facts, together with the social atmosphere of responsibility and punishment, make it very easy for the patient to regard the illness as retribution. And apparently random punishment may actually *induce* a process of searching for the cause. (There is the example, often quoted in the United States, of the school of parenting in which you randomly and periodically punish your child on the assumption that if you don't know what the child has done wrong it's a fair bet that the child does!) This process of searching the past in order to find out what has caused the illness is very common, and tends to be most pronounced when the illness is severe. I've seen it many times in patients hearing bad news, whether it's a diagnosis of cancer or multiple sclerosis or any other major illness. They feel a need to identify something they've done that may have caused the illness; the system of reward and punishment does, at least, make a kind of sense of the illness, whereas an illness that has nothing to do with the type of life you've led, that is unassociated with voluntary acts, does seem to be senseless and to insult the moral codes that we live by.

There are some people who capitalise on the inherent sense of guilt. I once listened to a talk by a representative of a fairly well-known alternative medicine centre in Britain at which they held the totally unproven view that every person's cancer is caused by that individual's psychological stresses. This representative said 'The first thing we do when we meet a new patient with breast cancer is to say, "What is it that you have done in your life to cause your breast cancer?" ' Since there is no evidence whatsoever to show that individual stresses do cause breast cancer, I became extremely angry and pointed out that this approach was certain to add large amounts of guilt to a patient's already heavy suffering.

So guilt emerges first because the patient sees the illness as a judgement on her previous life. Second, the guilt is amplified because the threat of death telescopes the future and puts a tremendous pressure on the patient and her family.

By 'telescoping the future' I mean that any life-threatening illness immediately reduces the time-scale by which we all work. Reducing the time-scale puts a sense of urgency into any unfinished business. All of us have unfinished business hanging over our heads: we all have unresolved arguments with friends or relatives, little or big things that we have done that are a bit selfish or aggressive, or in some way unworthy of the way we would like to behave. While we are enjoying good health we may carry that list with us assuming that we have sufficient time to sort it all out later. The threat of illness reduces that 'later' to 'soon' and imparts a sense of a deadline for the things we have not done. So when a person with a normal list of unfinished business suddenly becomes a patient with a limited future, it is easy to see how a sense of guilt about that unfinished business appears as if from nowhere.

It also follows from this that people will only feel guilty if they have sensitivity about their actions and other people's feelings and reactions to them. If a person upsets or offends other people and has no intention of repairing the damage, or any desire to do so, then that person is unlikely to experience guilt. In the same way in which fear requires imagination, so guilt requires sensitivity. The knowledge that she has sensitivity does not compensate for the feeling of guilt, nor will it abolish that guilt, but it is something worth pointing out to someone whom you are trying to support. Guilt may not have a *purpose* as such, but it certainly does signal some positive qualities in the sufferer.

Your Feelings

The emotions you may experience can best be considered under three headings:

1. *Feelings 'in sympathy' with the patient.* By this I mean that you may experience feelings that reflect or resonate with what your friend is feeling. He feels angry and you feel his anger, or he is in despair and your feelings reflect *his* despair.

2. *Your own feelings about the patient's illness.* These feelings may, of course, be quite independent of what he is going through. For instance, he may be in a state of accepting the inevitability of death, and you may be angry; or you may be in despair while he is feeling optimistic (inappropriately by your assessment), and so on.

3. *Your reactions to what the patient is expressing.* Here I am talking about your role as 'target' for the patient's feelings. This applies particularly to anger, which might easily be directed at you, but many of the patient's emotions will produce separate emotional responses inside you, and we need to think about those too.

Before I move on to work through this list, let us think for a moment about *why* you might experience very strong feelings. The central component is the sense of impending loss. It does not matter what kind of relationship you have with the patient, whether he is spouse, child or friend. Your sense of loss will depend on its closeness, past and present, not on whether you are first cousins or squash partners. By and large, relationships are based on a sense of trust and reliance, however intermittent. This means that the threat of the end of one participant's life means a great change in that trust and reliance. It also means the end of the survivor's emotional investment, the end of all that caring and all that depending on each other. This is a painful concept to accept, and to some extent it will be the root cause of your own pain.

Having recognised, then, that the depth and severity of the emotions you experience depend mainly on the closeness of your relationship and the realisation that it will end, we can move on to look at some of these feelings in more detail.

Reflecting the patient's feelings

You will experience some emotions solely *because* the patient is feeling them. Whether the emotion is anger, depression, denial, fear or any other (with the possible exception of guilt, which is probably always an individual's emotion exclusively), you are going through it with the patient. Psychologists and psychiatrists use the words 'empathy' and 'sympathy' about these feelings. There are strict definitions of empathy and sympathy, but they are not useful in this context. What is important is that you recognise which of your feelings are of this type. In other words, when you find yourself angry or depressed or afraid, you should ask yourself, 'Why am I feeling this way?' If the answer is, 'Because my friend is feeling this way,' then you can help focus on your *friend*'s emotions. If, on the other hand, the feelings are arising from something in your *own* emotional make-up and attitude, then you should try to be aware of this so that you don't thrust or project your own reactions on to the patient.

What I'm saying, then, is that you need to recognise sympathetic feelings (by which I mean those feelings inside you that coincide with the patient's feelings), and understand that they are a natural response and almost always a useful way of adding your support. You should not fight them but recognise them.

Your own feelings

As a friend of the person facing death, but as someone who will survive the patient, you will have your own feelings about your friend's illness and impending death. Not only are you entitled to have your own feelings, but it would also be impossible for you *not* to have your own feelings about what's going on. The only important thing is for you to sort out – as far as you are able – which feelings *are* your own, so that you don't confuse them with the patient's feelings.

So what are the feelings you may experience? Well, simply as an involved onlooker you will almost certainly feel considerable sadness about the impending loss. There is very little that anyone can say to reduce sadness, because the death of someone we love, even if it is a release from physical suffering, is sad. It needs to be stressed that the part of you that feels the sadness is the part of you that cares, and that's a part of your personality that's worth cherishing even though it is causing you pain at this particular time. (As one commonly quoted phrase puts it, 'The part that hurts is the part that counts.')

You may also experience relief that you do not have the illness yourself. A sense of relief is very common, and most relatives are ashamed of it, feeling that it is an unnatural and unworthy reaction. The opposite is the case. The feeling of relief is virtually a reflex response to the threat that you observe affecting your friend's future. During the moments in which you experience it, you cannot pretend that it does not exist. It is often helpful to discuss that feeling with someone else close to you. It can be difficult to discuss it directly with the patient unless you have reached a level of intimacy with her in which she will not be hurt or offended by being reminded of the fact that you are being spared.

In addition to the sadness and the pain, you may go through exactly the same emotions *in your own right* as the patient does. You may go through shock and disbelief of your own ('I can't believe that my sister has cancer'), or true denial ('Derek looks so well – they must have made a mistake'), even if your sister or Derek have taken the news on board themselves. Similarly, you may go through cycles of despair and depression. Everything I've said already about the patient's reactions to the threat of death may apply equally to you. However, some of these reactions may be slightly different in the supporting friend or relative, so I shall now consider these differences.

Anger and blame

You may experience anger of your own. The target of your anger may be (as the patient's may be) the healthy world, the uncaring universe, the unfairness of the system, the insensitive or incompetent health professionals (whether genuinely so or not). Or – and this is really important – you may be angry at the patient himself. This kind of reaction, feeling angry at the patient *because* he is ill and dying, is common.

At first sight, feeling angry at a sick person whom you are trying to help may seem bizarre, but it happens often. It is particularly likely to happen when the relative is in some way dependent on the patient. The most common example is when the patient is the family's breadwinner and the supporter is the dependent husband or wife. The dependent (healthy) spouse often comes to resent the disruption of family life and may have major fears about what will happen to her or him after the patient has died. She or he becomes angry and often incommunicative with the patient *because the patient is the bearer and the representation of the illness, and the source of the disruption and threat.*

The fact that you understand and recognise the source of this anger will not stop it happening. For example, Ruth Gallop remembers very clearly a time when her husband Leslie was terminally ill, their son was very young and they had to travel overseas. As Ruth put it, 'I found that I was so angry that I couldn't talk to Leslie for a time.' But why was she angry? And why angry with him? 'Because, by being ill, the sick person seems to be letting the healthy partner down. . . . Plans cannot be made, or if they are made, fall through. . . . Nothing seems sure or secure . . . and all the emotional investment you've made in the other person seems about to be lost.' Ruth was a skilled psychotherapist, and yet the load of anger she experienced was so heavy that it almost caused a communication breakdown between her and Leslie. Fortunately, she was able to talk to other therapists about the problem and by getting help in seeing what was going on was able to deal with the very strong feelings, and was able to start talking normally with Leslie again.

Ruth's experience is not a rare one. For instance, a spouse may resent the disability of the sick family member very intensely, and react in ways that to the outsider look like cruelty. Relatives and friends of patients may, for example, be slow in bringing pain-killers, find that they can't visit the patient in hospital, deny the patient signs of caring and affection (including sex) – and all with excuses that vary from the plausible to the flimsy. These are not signs that the friend doesn't really care – they're outward signs of the anger and resentment that he feels when his friend is ill. I've seen these reactions very often. Here are just a few examples of what some friends and relatives have said:

'This is not what I agreed to take on when I married him.'

'Why can't she get healthy again?'

'He's doing it deliberately.'

'She's not trying any more.'

'He's enjoying the attention.'

'I have to work like a slave, and he gets all the sympathy and attention.'

'All my life I've been looking after someone – first it was my parents, then my children, now it's him. When is it going to be my turn to have someone look after me?'

These feelings are not unnatural, nor, usually, are they untrue. As the healthy member of the family or circle, you may well find yourself experiencing great resentment against this illness that you *didn't* expect and don't want, which *is* destroying your relationship and your life-style and which *is* simply unfair and unjust. There are so many reasons for resenting the illness and resenting the threat of death and loss. The real problem is that because the patient often seems to be the cause of all the resentment, he or she becomes the target of it.

Naturally, understanding the causes of your own feelings of resentment doesn't wipe them out at a stroke. But if you are able to recognise some of these feelings in yourself, then you may be able to think them through and even talk about them with other people, including perhaps the patient. This will help you to get a handle on them instead of letting them overwhelm you and get in the way of your supporting the patient.

If you can manage to ask yourself, 'Why am I getting angry?' then you may give yourself enough distance to see that it's to do with the disease and the awful impact of the disease on you and the patient – and that your *real* anger shouldn't be aimed at the patient.

Of course, if you're feeling really angry it may be almost impossible to check yourself. You may find yourself exploding in anger or resentment and saying things that afterwards seem very unfair and unkind. If that does happen (and it *isn't* all that rare, believe me!), then the best thing to do is think about it afterwards, go back to the patient when you've cooled down and try to describe what you were feeling. Even if those feelings were not actually 'good' or 'beneficial', nevertheless it's much better to talk about it than simply to let the outburst pass as if it had not happened, which will weaken trust and place a block between the two of you.

Another reason relatives blame the patient for the illness is to shore up their own hope that 'it couldn't have happened to me'. We all hope we're not going to get ill ourselves. We constantly look for things the patient did wrong that would make the disease 'his own fault'. The implication is that if we (the onlookers) don't make that mistake we'll be all right. ('I've always looked after myself – unlike poor old Richard – so I'll be all right').

In my own case, when I developed the condition that made me so ill (which was an inherited auto-immune problem and not caused by anything other than being born with certain genes), people very close to me took the opportunity to lecture me about everything I'd always done wrong ('and now look what's happened!'). Everybody had their own diet plan I should have followed, their sleeping patterns I never took examples from, bowel training that I studiously ignored, and so on. The relatives who gave me these lectures did it out of a genuine sense of love and concern for me and with an added sense of fright and shock that this could happen to someone close. It was this that pushed them into looking for reasons why it happened to me and not to them. I must add that it is very boring to have to listen to this moralising, however well-intentioned. The last thing a patient wants to hear is what he or she should have been doing since birth to avoid getting ill.

You should therefore limit the advice you give. When you are close to someone who is ill, do not make his plight worse by burdening him with your views on the way he should have lived his life. It may make *you* feel better but it won't help him at all. It may well distance you from the illness, which may be some relief for you, but it'll also distance you from the patient, which makes you less of a help.

Now, of course, some diseases *are* caused by what the patient does, directly or indirectly. Smoking causes lung cancer (or 97 per cent of it, anyway); prolonged excessive consumption of alcohol causes liver damage, and so on. But if you want to help your friend, do not lecture him. Do not raise the subject unless he does, and do not use the weakness of the patient's position for any self-righteous teaching. It will not be helpful, and, even if it is correct, it is too late.

Fear

You will have your own fears, and the precise nature of those fears will depend in part on the nature of your relationship with the patient. You may be frightened of being left alone, of being helpless, of cracking up and failing to cope, of being a hindrance to the patient when you should be a help, of trying to live without the patient afterwards and failing, and so on. You may have very vivid fears of being left isolated, of never having any real life after bereavement, of 'going mad' without him or her. Or you may have very practical fears about what's going on at present: What if the illness carries on for a very long time until you are both exhausted and drained and come to resent or even hate each other? However shameful these feelings may appear, most friends and relatives have them, and they're not unnatural or a sign of some callous streak in your personality.

Sometimes, as the patient comes to accept death, the relatives may become more frightened rather than less. I remember a couple in their late thirties. The wife, Deborah, was a very beautiful woman who had a very aggressive cancer that had relapsed. Her husband, Harry, was an extremely pushy and aggressive man, and although the situation was hopeless he simply was not ready to accept it. The problem was that Deborah *knew* she was dying and wanted to talk. Harry would listen to anything she said except on the subject of death. For several days I felt caught between them. She wanted to hear the truth and to talk about it, he didn't want the facts out in the open. The problem was that Deborah had some important things she wanted to say to Harry, and she asked me if I'd help her.

What happened in the interview, at first, threw me completely. Every time Deborah started to talk about the fact that she was dying Harry stopped her physically. First he pushed her fruit juice at her and put the straw into her mouth. Then it was a sandwich. Then when she tried again to say that she knew it was the end, he started kissing her on the mouth while she was still talking. His behaviour was so out of the ordinary that I was rather embarrassed, as was Deborah. Then it occurred to me that Harry – for all his strength and push – was scared. He was very frightened of Deborah's impending death, and the fact that she clearly wasn't frightened made him feel even more ill at ease.

Once we started talking about what *he* was afraid of, things got much easier. Harry was so used to pushing everybody else around that it was hard for him to face up to the fact that there were things even *he* was afraid of. But it is a common enough problem, and one that you can watch out for in yourself. If you are afraid, try to recognise it as honestly as you can. It may help you to get a grip on the fear that may be driving your anger and your frustration.

The list of fears that you may experience is long and personal. You may find that your fear manifests itself as panic, or as anxiety attacks, or even as anger.

When you get feelings of fear you should ask yourself, 'What is it precisely that I am afraid of?' Try to assemble a list of the things of which you are most afraid; some of them will be things that may happen to the patient and some will be things that may happen to you. The more closely you look at your fears, the less dreaded they will appear. Of course no amount of thinking can ever abolish fears entirely. You are going to lose your friend and that in itself is something unknown and fearful. All these exercises can do is reduce the scale of the fear, you will then handle it better and be more able to help your friend.

Guilt (yours)

A friend's guilt is caused in part by the same mechanism that makes the patient feel guilty: 'death is the punishment for which you must have committed a crime'. However, another contributory factor is the very common feeling that you have not been as close a friend or relative as you might have been. I think both of these causes are quite common and both can be very powerful. And both can be expressed as anger.

I remember one family particularly well in which the burden of guilt resting on the son of the patient was a major driving force in controlling his behaviour. The patient, Ivy, was in her late sixties when I was first asked to see her. She was very seriously ill, but there was a good chance her tumour would respond to chemotherapy (which it later did). She was an immigrant from eastern Europe and, to coin a phrase, she 'had a certain way with her'. She was incredibly stubborn and obstinate, and she had a strong desire to be in control of everything. But she was also very endearing and once she was sure I understood who was boss (her) we got on very well. The problem was her son.

Bob was in his early forties, and was – as he told me in the first few seconds of our interview – a 'big-shot lawyer'. The interview was somewhat stormy to begin with. He gave me a combination of the Spanish Inquisition and the Headmaster's Speech to the Way-ward Pupil. My knowledge of cancer treatments was probed in detail and I was also made to understand that for anything I did wrong I would be answerable to Bob. During this speech, Bob worked himself into a state of anger. I listened for a time, then I started asking about how Bob actually got on with his mother. I told him that I found her quite difficult to understand and get along with. I made it very clear that I was certain Bob had been a good son, and that she was probably quite a difficult mother at times and was very apt to criticise. Once Bob realised that *I* wasn't going to criticise him (in the way his mother always did), and that I didn't think he should feel guilty about his mother, he relaxed, and the big-shot lawyer façade faded. He told me quite openly that he was very used to being shouted at (which was why he was shouting at me) and had been feeling very guilty about his mother and her illness. Could it have been detected earlier if he'd visited her more often? In this case the answer was no. Would the treatment have been easier if she'd been living with him? No for her and no for him. Should he have been doing more? No, because however much he did, her usual way of communicating was to be dis-satisfied with some aspect, but that didn't mean he was a bad son. In the end, all three of us got along very well. She was quite happy grumbling as long as we respected her; Bob was happy as long as we knew he was a good son really; and I was quite glad that nobody was shouting at me.

I remember that family well because of the drama they created around them. Although it did have some slightly funny aspects (which Ivy and Bob realised even while they were in the middle of it), the guilt element is a serious problem. Sometimes, as in that family, the relatives actually feel more guilt than the patient. Often, it is because that's the way things were before the illness began and that is the way things will continue during it.

The sense of guilt is heightened by the spotlighting effect I mentioned earlier. We all have rows and arguments, and are used to having differences and then making up again. But if one day the row were followed by the onset of serious illness, we would be likely to feel very guilty. (One of the best descriptions of what that feels like is a story called 'A Fairy Tale of New York' by J. P. Donleavy, in which a man's wife dies suddenly, and, as he goes through the hard process of accompanying her coffin home, he thinks about some of the things he would have liked to have said had he known they had so little time. It is a very moving story, and very valuable without being overly sentimental.)

Curiously enough, the people who are most likely to feel guilty are children. If a parent is taken ill, the children may feel that it's because of something they did ('Maybe if I'd always tidied my room like Mum said, she wouldn't have died and left me'), and this is something I'll deal with in greater detail in Chapter Eleven.

Finally, you may feel guilt because you are going to survive and the patient is not. This sensation, sometimes called 'survivor guilt', is normal whenever we are threatened by the loss of somebody very close. It is most intense when the patient is a child, but in many relationships the relative or friend feels guilt because he is a powerless bystander. This, too, is a normal reaction to impending loss.

Your reactions to what the patient is expressing

We can now consider your own feelings, not as an observer of the patient, but as the target of the patient's emotions. It is always hard to be the supporter of the patient and the target or whipping-boy at the same time. Your friend is going through a series or a mixture of different emotions, some coherent and understandable, some contradictory and reflex, and at various stages these may be directed at you. While you are trying to support and help the patient and trying to stay close, you may well be the target for some of her moods and feelings – and the closer you are, the more likely you are to be the target.

You may be the target for anger because you're healthy and you're going to survive her death. You may be the target for denial, if the patient can make you join her in pretending the illness doesn't exist. You may be the target for guilt, since people who are feeling guilty can often reduce that feeling by making other people feel guilty. And you may be the target for despair – the patient may use despair as a weapon to beat you. You may be asked (or almost compelled) to witness anger directed at other people, for example nurses or doctors, and may be dragged in to referee and to support the patient's side of any dispute. All of these things can happen, and they are hard on you.

The key to being an effective supporter of the patient is to maintain a balance between staying close enough to her to understand what she is going through, and keeping back enough so that you do not trade blow for blow in direct confrontation. That balance is easier to describe than to achieve. You can make it a little easier for yourself if you keep on trying to imagine what it feels like for the patient. Look again at the example of the options I illustrated at the end of Chapter Two ('I'm dying and you're no help'). If your friend gets angry and tells you to get lost, even in the heat of the moment when you most feel like doing precisely that, ask yourself, 'Why is she being like this? What is she going through?' It might help to throw a switch in your own mind and take you off the family-row track on to one that brings you closer together.

What I have just said is the counsel of perfection. Much of the time you will feel enraged or frustrated or desperate, and from time to time you will not only feel like hitting back but will do so. It is impossible to control your every response and you should not try, but if you are aware of the possible options you will be able to reduce the number of times that the situation degenerates into a confrontation.

In summary, then, what I've been trying to do is help you unpick the strands of your own feelings – where they come from and what they mean. If they start from the feelings of your friend, it will help to be aware of that so that you can concentrate on your friend. If they are your own feelings about what's happening to your friend, then it is important to know that too; if they're helpful emotions you can share them, and if they're unhelpful you can try to filter them out. If your feelings are reactions to being the target, then you need to recognise that too, so that you can support instead of fight.

A Guide to Giving Support

Supporting someone who is just coming to grips with the threat of his or her illness requires both practical and emotional help. In general, the major impact early in the diagnosis is emotional. You can and should offer practical support (see Chapter 10), which may be of great value early in the process, even if the patient is feeling physically well. Offers of practical help are welcome at that stage and will have an emotional and symbolic worth to the patient.

After you have followed the steps outlined in Chapter 10, you may find the following approaches to the emotional aspects of your relationship useful.

General guidelines

1. *See where you fit in*. Do not rush in and take over. Go cautiously at first to find out where you can be of greatest help.

2. *Expect variability*. As I have mentioned already, your friend's mood and outlook will change from day to day. This is neither his fault nor yours; if you expect it, you will not be put off balance when it happens.

3. *Expect repetition*. People coping with major psychological stress often feel the need to go over the same ground time and time again. If you can, go along with it.

4. *Follow the patient's agenda, not your own*. Try not to start your support with a programme in mind, but try to feel your way. It is often unhelpful to go in to see a friend with a list of things they 'simply have to do' – whether you are suggesting faith healers, relaxation techniques, new diets, or anything else. See what the patient is already doing before you step in.

5. *Do not equate activity with support*. Many times the things you *do* for the patient will be helpful, sometimes they will not. Do not rush around getting second and third opinions unless the patient wants you to.

6. *Get informed – but don't become a world expert*. This is a guideline that you will meet time and time again in later chapters. It is extremely important that you learn enough about the medical situation to help constructively. Do not become an expert in your own right, catching the patient in a conflict of opinions.

I have already outlined approaches to some of the emotions you will encounter. What follows now are some additional guidelines directed at specific responses.

Helping with denial

Supporting someone who is going through denial is not easy. You are caught between two difficult choices. If the patient is ignoring obvious signs of the serious nature of the disease and says something like, 'I'll be better in no time, won't I?' you have few choices. If you agree with the statement, then you're endorsing a statement that isn't true. This will lead to trouble when the patient doesn't get visibly better. If, on the other hand, you say, 'No, you won't be getting better,' you are casting yourself as the person who takes away hope, and the adversary of the patient. Furthermore, if you take it on yourself to answer the question, you're also subliminally allowing yourself to be set up as a figure of authority, which will make life even more difficult for you later.

The first point to remember is that denial is powerful (as in the examples of the doctors with cancer) and you cannot simply override the patient's denial mechanisms by forcing the true facts down his throat. This does not mean that you have to accept openly his interpretation of the situation. There are ways of exploring the way someone is feeling without attacking their viewpoint. For instance you can try a 'what if . . .?' approach, which will allow the patient to think about the *possibility* of not getting better in the abstract, without having to admit at that minute that things are looking bad.

Or you can ask about the medical facts. Here are just a few possible ways forward:

> The patient says something like:
> *'I am going to get better, aren't I?'*
> ↓
> You have several choices:

You could say:
↓

'Of course you are.' – a
direct response that will
reduce your credibility
when things don't go well
later.
or
'No, you're not.' – a direct
response that makes you
appear cruel and adver-
sarial.

Or you could say:
↓

*'What have the doctors told
you?'*
or
*'I hope you will, but it might
not happen.'*
or
*'I'd like that, but perhaps we
ought to see what happens.'*
↓

All of these leave open the
possibility that things will
get worse, and allow you to
continue to be supportive.
↓

They also allow you to
raise the question, later:
*'Should we make some plans
for what to do if you don't get
better?'*

Helping with despair

Remember that despair means loss of hope. Remember also that,
although hope of cure and healthy life may not be yours to grant,
there are realistic hopes that are in your power to offer. The central
principle of coping with someone's loss of hope is that you should
never rush in to fill the vacuum with false hopes. Promising things
that cannot be delivered simply weakens your own credibility as a
friend and devalues your currency as a supporter. You will appear
less reliable and will discourage your friend from trusting you and
leaning on you later when he may need you most.

1. *Stick as closely to reality as possible.* By this I mean that you should
never promise anything if you think it will not happen. Patients
often say things like, 'I feel awful – things have to improve soon.'
This kind of statement seems to plead for an optimistic reply, and it
seems almost unnaturally cruel to deny that plea. But it's important to remember that those things are not yours to promise – and
promising things you can't deliver will simply make you appear
untrustworthy in the long run. By telling a person that something

is not mine to promise (a phrase I find useful in clinical practice), I can let him know that I would *like* to be able to make him better, that I hear his *hope* to get better, but that I am not unrealistic and that I have limitations. It allows me to be honest and realistic without seeming to withdraw from the person and without appearing to crush all hope.

2. *Acknowledge the way the patient feels.* Allow her to say how rotten she feels. Listen to it and take it on board. In other words, just *be* there, stay close. If you can't think of anything to say, it may be because there is nothing to say; just stay there with her – hold her hand if you don't feel awkward, or put your hand on her arm or shoulder. Despair isn't something you can fix or banish, but simply staying with the person during the worst of it, and not withdrawing or recoiling, is a great thing to do.

3. *Reinforce genuine hopes.* There are hopes that can be achieved (after the patient realises that you have understood how bad he's feeling and have not dismissed his despair). It is possible, for example, to relieve pain in at least 90 per cent of patients with incurable cancer. If you know that, then you will know that it is realistic to hope for relief from pain. It is also realistic to hope, in the great majority of cases, that the dying person will be able to maintain his dignity and respect in the process. We'll talk about that further in Chapter 7, but for now just keep in mind that if this is a major concern of the patient, the hope is realistic. Most important, as relative or friend, you can promise that you won't abandon the patient. You can tell the person that no matter how rough things get, you will be there. If you've never said anything like that in your life, you will have no idea how comforting it can be. The fear of being abandoned near the end is a big fear with most patients – and the hope that you'll stay by them is crucial and realistic.

With these three kinds of hope in mind, you will probably find that you can weather the patches of despair with the patient and that in doing so your contact and bond will strengthen rather than weaken (which is what would happen if you brought only false hope).

So far, then, we've dealt with the initial shock of the diagnosis on the patient, and the ripples that spread through you and other members of the family and circle of friends. Now I shall move on to consider the impact of the continuing illness – the feelings that go along with 'being ill'.

6

Being Ill

I have called the second stage of the transition from health to acceptance of dying 'being ill', and it is not an easy job to define it accurately. I am referring to the stage after the initial shock of diagnosis, but before the patient really *knows* that the end is near. In other words, the stage before the patient accepts the *inevitability* of death in the near future. As I have said, human emotions don't divide neatly into stages, so this second stage – 'being ill' – can begin very soon after diagnosis (or may even have begun before it) and may go on right to the end of the illness if the patient never really reaches the stage of accepting his imminent death.

This phase is characterised by two major factors: illness and uncertainty. The uncertainty is painful in itself and the constant fluctuations of hope and despair can be very wearing on the patient and friends (as Michael Frayn wrote: 'I can stand the despair. It's the hope I can't bear'). What really matters is trying to sort out what's going on during this sometimes uneasy phase. The threat of death is very prominent (but not imminent) in the patient's life, and it is materially affecting the quality of that life.

The Patient's Feelings

As the illness progresses, all the emotions that we discussed in Chapter 5 continue. There will often be anger, fear, guilt, and resentment over loss of control, and so on. Generally, the major shocks may fade as some adjustments are made, but there will often be minor shocks, particularly if new disabilities or symptoms develop. Denial becomes a bit more difficult (though some patients will maintain it nonetheless) and depression becomes more common.

We can best think about the experiences of a patient in this stage by splitting them up into two kinds: first, the physical symptoms caused by the disease, and second, the impact of these symptoms on the person's life and emotions.

The physical illness

As regards the physical symptoms, serious illnesses vary to a vast degree – from some illnesses that rapidly advance and paralyse, quickly rendering the patient incapable of most independent activities, to others that may in the early stages cause no impairment of function at all.

Most people have an image of a serious or life-threatening illness as one that instantly renders the patient gravely ill and totally incapacitated. Although this does happen (infrequently, in fact), usually it *isn't* sudden and the patient's physical condition deteriorates gradually, or stepwise. So for you, as friend or family member, it's most important that you realise that things do change and that the changes take place over a period of time, which is usually only partly predictable.

Many patients will be feeling fairly well at the time of diagnosis. This is because many serious diseases develop relatively slowly and nowadays most people consult doctors early and tend not to ignore symptoms for long periods of time. However, feeling well when you know you've got a serious disease is a difficult state to be in. Although, obviously, it's good not to have major physical symptoms and good to be able to perform a reasonable range of daily activities, it does often make it very difficult to get to grips with the seriousness of the situation. As one patient put it to me, 'I can't seem to get my mind round it.' Patients often say to me, 'But I feel so well,' and even more frequently express their frustration when well-meaning relatives and friends say things like, 'But you look so well!' 'As if,' the patients say, 'I have to *prove* to them that I've got a serious illness.'

So, if there are few physical symptoms, this is beneficial in the sense that it gives friends and family time with the patient – time that can be utilised to the full – but it is also somewhat baffling, like a 'phoney war', which makes the illness and the threat of death even more unreal.

If the early part of the illness is like that, it may last for some time. Usually the patient's condition deteriorates by degree. As one elderly woman said to me, 'I've gradually changed from a person to a patient, haven't I?' Some of the hundreds of possible physical problems may develop in this period. Usually they do not go away – or if they go away temporarily, they don't go away 'properly', which means that the patient can't put them out of her mind totally. This feeling, of having continuous physical symptoms, or the threat of them, is what I call 'the grind of being ill'.

The grind

In describing what it feels like in the 'being ill' stage, many patients have told me that their illness has a sort of physical presence in their lives, like an unwanted and uninvited guest sitting at the dinner table, making normal life and conversation difficult and strained. My own experience, even though it lasted less than two years, taught me how quickly the illness becomes, quite literally, 'part of the family', and how quickly serious physical symptoms such as pain, loss of appetite and nausea can drain the colour out of life, leaving the patient and family in a sort of sallow, monochrome world.

It might be worth trying the following mental exercise to help you to get an image of what 'the grind' is like for, say, a patient who has the nondescript but very common experience of simply feeling ill, feeling 'lousy' or 'fifth-rate', or suffering from (to use the correct medical word) *malaise*. Try to imagine it in the following way. Think for a moment about what it feels like when you get flu. You know that second-day-of-flu feeling when you feel simply rotten, when everything hurts or is uncomfortable and when you can hardly do anything. Getting up for a cup of tea or a visit to the bathroom is a major undertaking, and you could hardly imagine doing both of these things within an hour of each other. We have all had that – and felt very sorry for ourselves, but we've also known that the feeling would pass and we would be back to normal in a week.

Now imagine that this second-day-of-flu feeling does not go away, and you are feeling just as bad at the end of a week. Imagine how you would feel at the end of the second week. Then imagine it for a month. A month – you are not back at work, and nobody can tell you when you're going to get back to work. If at all. Now add to that a regular series of tests – X-rays, blood tests, scans – and perhaps treatments with drugs by tablet or injection, or with radiotherapy or surgery. On top of that there may be all the uncertainty about the future. . . .

I am not suggesting that you perform this mental exercise as some form of scare tactic. I am trying to get you to visualise the reality of chronic illness and the continued frustration that so many patients (although not all) go through – and which so many families and friends never really understand.

During this phase, support from friends and family is at a premium. When the shock of the diagnosis is new ('Isn't it terrible? Brian's just been told that . . .'), the circle may well flock round with (welcome) sympathy and support. But as the illness continues and nothing much changes, friends and family do tend to fade away into the background. Nothing much seems to be happening, the need seems to be less urgent. But just because nothing is changing doesn't mean that needs are less – in fact it is often the opposite. In this 'grind' phase, the patient and the family and friends may *all* get bored and frustrated. You need to be aware that this is a common and normal feeling at this stage.

To summarise then, the most important aspects of the physical illness (after the initial shock) are: the loss of control and daily activity; the wearing, grinding effect that this causes when it doesn't get better; and the uncertainty about the future.

The emotional impact of physical symptoms

So far, I have been building up a picture of some of the physical feelings your friend may be going through. But there are many other ways in which the illness can affect the quality and style of your friend's life. I shall mention some of them briefly but it is not possible to give a complete list, first because there are so many kinds of physical problems, and second because the impact of any given physical problem depends on that person's previous life-style in health.

Let me explain that in greater detail. If I broke a leg and needed to wear a plaster cast for a month, that would be a nuisance and would irritate me, but because I am not very athletic and because I could just about manage my job in medicine it would not be a disaster. If, on the other hand, I were a professional tennis player or an actor, it *would* be a catastrophe. In practice, that is what happens: the impact of the illness depends on the way the patient arranges his priorities. (In my own case, for example, when it seemed quite likely during the two years of my illness that I would not be able to walk easily again, it was not difficult to investigate a sub-speciality of medicine that could be done sitting down. In arranging for that eventuality I wasn't being brave, I was just lucky that I wasn't totally dependent on my physical abilities.) This means that if you want to know what is bothering the patient most of all about their physical situation, you have to ask them.

As another example, consider an operation for breast cancer. Depending on the size of the tumour, the size of the breast and several other factors, the patient might have part of the breast removed ('segmental mastectomy', sometimes also called 'partial mastectomy' or 'lumpectomy'), or the whole breast removed. The impact of the operation varies enormously. There may be a very serious alteration in the way the patient thinks about her body; it may make her feel that she is no longer sexually attractive; it may remind her of the diagnosis each time she undresses; the operation site may frighten her; it may frighten her partner, and either or both of them may become depressed or anxious. The way in which one particular person reacts to the operation will depend on her personality – on the way she thinks about her body and her image before the illness (Is she very self-conscious? Does she set a great deal of store by her physical appearance?), her own sexuality (Is she secure or is she constantly needing to be reassured by different people that she is attractive?), her closeness to her partner and to her friends (Does she usually talk to people – including you – about things that bother her, or does she hide her feelings away and put on a show of being just fine?). All these things – which exist before the illness – will set the pattern for the impact of this operation on the individual person.

This means that it is very difficult to make accurate statements about the impact of an illness or an operation on an individual. For the different kinds of mastectomy operation that I've mentioned above, for instance, you might think that the smaller the operation, the less the impact. In fact that is not the case. Detailed psychological testing on patients who had had partial mastectomies showed that these women have the same chance of feeling very depressed and deeply upset by the operation as women who have had a whole breast removed.

I have used mastectomy as an example, but everything I have said applies to some extent to all physical symptoms. A colostomy (an operation in which an opening from the bowel is made in the abdominal wall requiring the patient to wear a drainage bag) may also upset people to different degrees. There may be problems with appearance and self-consciousness. The more fastidious a person is, the more he or she may be upset by not having total control of their bowel movements. If the patient has a long-term close partner, then a colostomy may not affect their sex life at all; if the patient is single and has had several shorter-term relationships, then a colostomy could drastically affect that life-style.

Other examples include loss of hair (as happens with several kinds of chemotherapy and with radiotherapy to the head), difficulty in walking (needing a cane or a wheelchair), a catheter (a thin tube put into the bladder to drain urine when the bladder does not work properly), pain, difficulty in breathing (perhaps requiring oxygen by mask or tubes in the nostrils), difficulty in eating, difficulty in talking (with diseases of the larynx or vocal chords), and many others.

The key to understanding all of this is that your friend is facing something that he can't completely control. He cannot have complete control over the physical symptoms, and that will upset him to a degree that depends on how much he *values* his ability to control everything in his life.

In summary, then, the physical illness is as individual as the person it affects. What matters is what is actually going on with your friend right now. What bothers him the most, and how close are you to him? How much does he want you to help and how much are you willing to do? If you are willing to get in close to your friend, then there are certain reactions that are quite common when the physical illness seems to be overwhelming. Perhaps the most important of these is the feeling that it is all hopeless, and that there is no point in even trying to carry on.

'What's the point?'

Most of us are surprisingly courageous in emergencies. Even people who think that they are 'not good at putting up with pain' are often unexpectedly good at coping with it in an emergency. However, a lot depends on what we make of the situation confronting us. Generally, our ability to cope with pain is quite good if we think it will not last long, but bad if we cannot see an end to the pain, and feel hopeless.

This means that whereas most people are quite good at dealing with an obviously short-lived pain, such as the pain of a healing operation scar, a broken limb or childbirth, when there is no end in sight to the suffering it is much more difficult for the patient to muster her strength and willpower.

What often happens is that the person going through the illness says something like, 'What's the point in carrying on?' A patient speaking to an audience of doctors at an international conference said, 'It's like a tunnel that we are asked to crawl through – except that when we've crawled all the way through it, all there is waiting for us is another tunnel, and more tunnels after that.'

That reaction is complex and extremely important. It is a mixture of emotion and reason. It may contain some despair – a feeling of loss of hope – but it may also contain a genuine and rational balancing of the benefits and costs of struggling against the disease, and a recognition that there genuinely is not much point in carrying on struggling. These are things that cannot be ignored but which you, as supporter of the person going through this illness, must take seriously. I don't think there's a single word to describe this deep and chronic 'what's the point?' feeling, but it is not an acute short-lived despair, nor a sudden suicidal urge to end it all, it is a gradual but total *darkening* of that person's view of the world. The light goes out, and the picture becomes a pervasive grey. This is very hard on the family and supporters, who often feel (rightly) that they're doing their utmost to brighten up the picture for the patient who has now 'gone sullen on them' and is unappreciative of their efforts.

Once again, there are no simple answers to this very serious kind of doubt. You cannot fix it or banish it instantly. But you can use the same approach that I mentioned in dealing with despair in Chapter 5, 'A guide to giving support', acknowledging the depth of your friend's feelings and offering those hopes that are realistic.

For the moment, then, let me summarise what the patient may be going through in the 'being ill' phase: the continuing emotions that began in the 'facing the threat' stage, plus the emotional impact of the physical illness, and uncertainty about the future. These emotions will, of course, rebound on you, so let us now look at some of the things you may be experiencing.

Your feelings

Now that you have an image of what the patient is going through, we can start thinking about you. During the 'being ill' phase there is a greater chance that your feelings will be out of step with the patient's feelings. It is during this stage that there is the greatest danger of major differences and gaps between you.

Your feelings that reflect the patient's feelings

As in 'facing the threat', you may easily pick up on what your friend is going through. You may find that you experience her anger and her frustration, and you may also find yourself feeling that there is no point in carrying on.

I won't dwell on this aspect of what you're going through, because the message is the same as before: you have to be aware of where the feelings originate. If what you are feeling is a direct reflection of what your friend is going through, then you need to recognise that. It will not cancel out the intensity of your feelings at a stroke, but it will help you to get them in perspective. For instance, if one day you are feeling really low and going through a 'what's the point?' phase, you might feel so bad that you don't want to go and visit your friend. If, when you think about it, you realise that this is because, at the last visit, your friend was in this state and you picked up on it, then that realisation may help you. By noticing that your feelings didn't actually start with you, you may be able to give yourself a bit of space and gain extra strength and stamina.

Your reactions to the patient's illness

In the 'being ill' phase, your reactions to the illness may be very intense and may create deep rifts and obstacles between you and the patient.

'To be totally honest,' a relative once said to me, 'the most awful think about a long serious illness is that it's frustrating, it's boring, and it's a drag.'

Everybody feels resentment and anger at some stage during a friend's serious illness, particularly if it is long. Angry thoughts and feelings occur which, in the cold light of day, would seem cruel and callous. Here are some examples of what relatives and friends of some of my patients have said about this phase:

'I don't know whether I can stand it any longer.'

'I can hardly bear visiting him any more.'

'It's getting to the stage when I almost wish she were already dead.'

'I seem to hate him because he's not getting better.'

'I've got my own life to live, you know.'

'I can hardly wait for it to be over, but that makes me feel terrible.'

'This is no kind of life we're leading.'

All these examples show that supporting a seriously ill person takes a major toll on the supporter. Your life-style may be affected as much as (or even more than) the patient's. You may be spending your time doing things you don't really want to do but have to do. The burden of the relationship may fall on your shoulders; you may not want it and you may resent it.

You cannot *help* feeling resentment. But you *can* help (both yourself and the patient) by recognising that you do feel some resentment and by not pretending that it does not exist. If you recognise that you are feeling this way, you can respond to the patient by saying something like, 'This is really tough, and I'm getting very bad tempered' (which is a way of *describing* your feelings) rather than 'You never do anything except lie there and grumble' (which is a way of *exhibiting* your feelings, and quite likely to lead to an argument).

Probably, you *will* resent the loss of your independence, you will feel the weight of the demands made on you and you will miss the fun you used to have together, and you will resent the illness. These feelings are very common and you should try hard to separate the resentment that you feel towards the illness from your feelings for your friend. Unfortunately, the patient is often the only person around to catch the blame. He is also the embodiment of the illness, so it is easy for you to shift the focus of your resentment and unhappiness straight on to him, adding to his problems as well as your own. Being forewarned is being forearmed: if you are aware of the tendency, then you can reduce its impact.

Anticipatory grief

During the illness, particularly if the patient and the friends and family are aware that the illness is ultimately fatal, you may not be able to stop yourself thinking about your friend's death. It is normal for this process to begin before death – both for the patient who mourns the coming end of life, and for you. This anticipatory grief may cause you to experience guilt during the illness and after the death if you do not realise that it is a normal process. I shall deal with this later in some detail, but at this stage I just want to indicate to you that an impending sense of loss is both common and natural.

A guide to giving support

In the 'facing the threat' stage, the emotional shock is massive. In the 'being ill' stage, problems are both emotional and physical, and that means that the sick person needs help on two levels: practical and emotional. It is always worth remembering that there is more than one way of offering help and support. For instance, if your friend is deeply depressed about, say, being bald from chemotherapy, you can certainly be kind and supportive and constant, but you can also take your friend out and help her to get a wig. So before we start looking at the tactics and approaches, let me state clearly that the first thing to do is to find out what the major trouble spots are and whether any of them can be fixed simply. If they can be fixed, then help to fix them.

1. *Assess the needs.* There isn't space in this book for me to give specific advice about the thousands of things that can be done for seriously ill and dying patients. Nor is this the right kind of book for that kind of important and detailed advice. There are many hundreds of booklets available to patients and their families that have all the details that make a vast difference in looking after, for

instance, a colostomy, or in the management of catheters, mastectomy counselling, selecting walking aids and chairs, aids for daily living, and so on. If you want to help your friend in some specific way, then there are many ways of starting out. You can begin by talking to the doctor and nurses looking after the patient, visiting the local cancer society or disease-orientated self-help groups, local information offices, local hospital volunteers and so on.

2. *Help your friend to make choices.* Physical and practical support is essential – and usually much appreciated – but, on the emotional level, things are often difficult. The 'being ill' stage will almost always involve choices and decisions for the patient: whether to undergo a course of treatment, whether to get a second opinion regarding surgery, whether the side-effects of therapy are tolerable when measured against the potential benefit, and so on. And you may be asked to support the patient as he faces up to these vitally important decisions and uncertainties. It is crucial that you accept that the patient *has the right* to make his choice. It is his choice, and you have to respect it even if it is not the choice you would make. You can help him to balance up the pros and the cons. You can help him to realise that he does have a choice, but you cannot – and must not – choose for him. If you do, you line yourself up for blame and responsibility for the outcome. It is often hard for family members to allow the patient freedom of choice, and often the pressure for a patient to persevere with treatment comes from the family, who do not themselves have to go through the side-effects. One patient, Ben, was in his early forties when he was diagnosed as having a cancer that was particularly resistant to therapy. In discussing the therapy with him, his doctor was fair and honest and made it clear that drug treatment had only a small chance of helping him.

The situation was tragic, and, to make it even worse, he and his wife had only just started a long-planned-for family, and their daughter was a few months old. Ben himself was clear in his own mind that he did not wish to go through a course of treatment that was most likely to be ineffective, and did not want to be made ill by the therapy during what might be his last chance to spend time with his daughter. His wife and some of her relatives felt differently. Ben was pulled in different directions. He told the doctor, 'I think I've got to have the chemotherapy for my family's sake.' But this decision clearly made him unhappy and uneasy.

His doctor, working together with John Martin, got the family together to talk about it. After a lot of discussion, the family realised that because *their* desire for Ben to live was so strong, they weren't ready to accept that he really was going to die, and that treatment really would not prevent his death. It was hard and painful for them to accept it, but when they did they understood that they had been putting an unfair pressure on Ben and that it was his right to make his own decisions.

In this example, it was quite hard for the family to accept Ben's right to choose – but if they had not done so, and if Ben had been a weaker person, he might have gone through treatment unwillingly and 'for the sake of others'. He would have resented those 'others' for making him do that. Instead of which, Ben and his family came to appreciate how much they all meant to each other.

3. *Explore what your friend really wants and means.* Often during treatment a patient may say something indicative of a deeply felt fear or anxiety. Consider a person who has a tumour in the bowel, feels fairly well and has relatively few symptoms. The X-rays show the tumour and the doctor recommends surgery which will result in a colostomy. The patient is talking to you about the decision and says, 'I'd rather be dead than have a colostomy.' What does she mean by that?

She may mean several different things, and some of what she means may actually be contradictory. She may mean, 'I'm not ready to face the fact that I have cancer of the bowel.' This is actually quite a common reaction and the thinking goes something like this: 'The doctor says I have a serious illness and need surgery. If I don't have surgery then I won't have to face the fact that I've got this disease.' In other words, refusing surgery is a way of denying the existence of the disease.

She may be afraid. Sometimes patients cannot say outright, 'I'm scared', so they say something that sounds quite brave. 'I'd rather be dead . . .' has overtones of 'I'm not afraid of death', but actually she may mean the exact opposite, and fear of dying may push her into this pose.

She may also genuinely and sincerely loathe the prospect and the inconvenience of surgery and a colostomy. She may earnestly wish that she didn't have to have it, and think that she can abolish it from view by comparing it to something even bigger: her own death.

She may be angry. Rage and rejection of the concept of a colostomy may be her way of raging against the disease. By rejecting the offered treatment, she is at least exercising some form of control over her situation, which may be a way of compensating for the fact that she has no control over the disease itself.

She may also be in despair. To see the words written on the page you'd think that 'I'd rather be dead than have a colostomy' was most likely to be a cry of despair, and that you should accept that the patient wants to die, and leave it at that. In practice, despair is rarely the most important component of that reaction.

What you can do is help the person in this crisis unpick the strands of her feelings. Get her to talk about what she means by what she's said. Does she really mean she wants to die? Or does she mean she's afraid? And, if she is afraid, what of? Dying? Surgery? Inconvenience? Pain? Or does she mean that she simply can't face the decision now? And, if that is the case, does she *have* to make that decision today, this minute? Does she have a few days or a week to decide? Does she need more information? Would it help to talk to the doctor some more, or to someone who's had the operation, or a colostomy expert (for example a person called a 'stoma nurse') who can answer the detailed questions?

If you can see what I'm saying about this kind of cry for help, then you'll see that 'I'd rather be dead than have a colostomy' is not a single monolithic statement that you have to accept or confront head-on. It's an emotional response that may contain a lot of different elements, and, if you stick close and help the person sort them out, you can approach a topic that you might previously have thought totally unapproachable.

7

The Last Stage

In the last stage of a terminal illness the patient may come to recognise the inevitability of death, and accept that it is going to happen in the immediate future. Some patients accept it early in the illness and others never accept it at all. And, among the health professions, some authorities feel that patients *must* accept it, while others feel that patients don't *have* to accept it openly, but that it is generally better for them and their friends if they do.

But what about you? What should you do about accepting the inevitability of your friend's death? When is it permissible for *you* to think that it's time to stop struggling, and time to prepare for the end? When should you stop asking other people about miracle cures in Mexico and special clinics in Switzerland? When is letting go permissible and not a sign that you don't care? And what happens after that?

Answering these questions is the main object of this chapter, and I shall start by talking about what acceptance means to the patient, and then what it means to you. Then I shall deal with some of the difficulties that occur before acceptance (including the need for second opinions and alternative medicines) and then the major factors that need to be considered after acceptance, such as the patient's last wishes, the living will, promises that you feel you ought to make, and what you may feel if you are not there at the final moment. Finally, I shall deal with the issue of euthanasia.

The patient's feelings

As acceptance grows (if it does), the patient usually feels sad and very often tender. Once the major uncertainties and the big struggles are seen to be over, there is usually more peace and less anger. By definition, I imply that in the final stage denial has disappeared, and that, if the patient is still showing a fair amount of denial, then they are not – emotionally – in the final stage.

Acceptance almost always brings true sadness (as opposed to depression). The patient is sad at the prospect of being parted from friends and family and leaving the enjoyable things of life. This sadness is natural. It is something that you can allow the person to express normally and which should not upset you, although it will make you feel sad as well.

Although sadness is the most natural feeling, not every dying person feels it. Some people – usually people with strong religious beliefs and a firm image of an afterlife – face the final stage with no sadness at all, but look forward to being reunited with those who have died before them. For the people who have this belief, it is an enormous comfort. They are generally very strong about the end of their life and able to communicate easily with their friends and family.

For most other people, sadness will be part of the final stage and the sadness itself contains grief. Many people at the end of their lives experience mourning. They are mourning for themselves, which is also a rational and normal process. They don't want to stop living and so they mourn, in exactly the same way as the surviving relatives mourn after their bereavement. If you realise that this is part of the process, you won't be upset when you see it.

As regards the way in which patients approach the end of their lives, one point is crucial. Most people die as they have lived. If, in your daily life, you're an easy, cheerful, coping kind of person, then you will probably approach the end of your life in the same way (provided you are kept free of pain or other major physical problems). If you are a neurotic or cantankerous sort, then that is probably the way you'll be at the end. Death-bed conversions are rare. Most of us, of course, are mixtures – a bit neurotic, a bit brave, a bit humorous, a bit grouchy – and most of us will meet our deaths with the same mixture of moods or traits.

Some deaths are so much in character that they seem to exemplify the person's life. One such was that of my favourite uncle, Barry, who was simply a great human being. He was funny and bright, he had a strong sense of social justice, he was good at his job and everybody in the family loved him. He had a quick temper but was equally quick to forgive and forget. He died young and I was with him when he died. Even in the last few hours of his life he still showed care and concern for all of us around him and was appreciative of all the help he was getting. I don't want to sound overly sentimental, although his death was an exceptionally deep experience for all of us, but the last thing he said was a joke. It was actually a very witty comment on something that was going on, but the real point was that at the very end of his life, Barry behaved as *himself*. I have never forgotten that. In fact, it was watching Barry cope with dying that gave me the feeling that death can happen with dignity and integrity and that it's a goal that we can try to help our friends achieve (and try to achieve ourselves when it's our turn). Barry kept going as Barry until he stopped, and he gave all of us with him the courage to try to do the same.

It should be your objective as friend and supporter – as it should be my objective when I'm looking after dying patients – to help him to let go of life *in his own way*. It may not be your way or the way you would like to see, and it may not be the way you read about in a book or magazine, but it's his way and consistent with the way he's lived his life. As members of the circle, you can and should help your friend achieve that.

On the subject of the last hours of someone's life, there are some medical aspects which may be of help to you. Most people die by slipping into a coma before the moment of death. It is not invariable. Obviously some deaths are sudden, a few are violent and a few are painful until the very end. The great majority of people, however, will slip into a state of unawareness in which those around them 'can't get through' to them. This phase may last a few minutes or hours before the death, or, in the case of brain damage or other problems, it may go on for days, weeks or months. The type of death portrayed on television or in films – in which the dying person is totally coherent one instant and dead the next – is not common.

Many survivors of near-dying experiences (including a very

famous account by Dr David Livingstone of his near-death after a lion attack) have described a sense of peace and tranquillity that comes as death appears to be close, and which removes pain and struggle. Although it may seem somewhat matter-of-fact, it appears that this sensation is actually caused by substances produced in the brain called endorphins, which are similar to a naturally produced form of major pain-killer. It also seems that many of the 'depersonalisation' experiences recounted by near-death survivors, in which they felt themselves moving outside their own bodies and felt they were observing the events going on from a remote position, are due to a lack of oxygen in a part of the brain called the temporal lobe. Similar experiences have been produced during certain special kinds of brain surgery in which the patient needs to be awake.

The end of life is quite often imbued with a special tenderness. Although death-bed transformations are not common, and a J. R. Ewing usually dies as a J. R. Ewing and not as a St Francis of Assisi, quite often patients do become more sensitive to their own emotions and those of the people around them. It is almost as if their ability to receive emotions improves or as if their 'emotional hearing' suddenly sharpens and heightens. Usually this is not a *new* side of their personality appearing, but rather an increased emphasis on the sensitivity that is already there. When this happens, it is good for the patient and the family.

Your feelings

As in the earlier stages, you may experience periods of quite intense sadness and anticipatory grief, and also anger and resentment. But in addition, as the illness seems to be moving into the final stage, many relatives and friends experience exhaustion, both emotional and physical. Sometimes, at moments when it seems as if you and the patient will be locked in this pain for ever, you may feel a sense of impatience. One woman, Anne, who had been married to her husband, Peter, for over twenty years told me about her feelings during his prolonged illness. He had many physical symptoms which meant Anne was always running up and down the stairs of their home. She put her feelings this way: 'One day I thought to myself "If you call out to have your pillow fixed once more, I'm going to hold it over your face. I can't take this for one more day.'''

The frustration that Anne had been experiencing sharpened into a sense of impatience, which is not a rare feeling for people looking after a dying person. Naturally it seems cruel and callous, but thoughts such as, 'I felt that if he wasn't dying, I'd kill him myself,' are common. It's like having a baby that cries all the time: most parents faced with this situation say (or think), 'One more minute of this and I'm going to hit this child.' Almost every parent *feels like that* at some time, but the number of parents who *do* hit their babies is very small. So it is with exhaustion and impatience. Almost every supporting relative has, at some time, thoughts of impatience, and ancitipates the end of the patient's life with some sense of relief. In the vast majority of cases, these thoughts are normal reflex reactions and not a sign that you've stopped caring.

Loss of control

You may experience loss of control. During the physical illness you may have been doing many things for the patient, and you may have been valuable and appreciated. As the patient nears the end, you may feel strong disappointment because you are losing control as the disease seems to take over. These feelings of impotence and frustration may show themselves as anger or withdrawal – you may subconsciously blame the patient and you may withdraw from her because you feel that so much of your previous emotional investment has been wasted. Again, being aware of these feelings and why they happen may allow you to step back and take a break so that you can get the whole situation in perspective again.

Differences in acceptance

When the patient reaches acceptance and is preparing himself for dying, you – and perhaps other members of the circle – may not be able to accept it. This difference in acceptance can create major difficulties. One patient of mine, Victor, was in his late twenties. He had a particularly aggressive form of liver disease that had been diagnosed about a year before I first met him. His family was South American and very close. His mother was distraught at Victor's declining health. Her own distress was made much worse because she depended on translators to tell her what doctors and nurses were saying about his condition. Victor and his sister were both highly intelligent and well educated, but there was a big difference between them: Victor was resigned to the fact that he was going to die, and his sister was not. She took him to an alternative medicine clinic and smuggled the drugs back with them on the plane. She continued to give him the drugs even during his last few days of life. Victor was too ill to care very much about this, and when John and I asked him about it, it was clear that it didn't disturb him greatly.

Two days before he died, Victor asked for a priest to give him the last rites. His sister and mother refused to allow it. It was an exceptionally difficult situation. They had no *right* to refuse him this sacrament, but, on the other hand, a screaming argument on the ward around a dying man was something we wanted to avoid. We discussed it at length with them, and pointed out that the most important person was Victor. We gave the family the space to say how much they wanted him to live. We pointed out that the last rites do not in themselves hasten death, but that denying him what he wanted was unfair and cruel. After much discussion they relented and were able to reach the same state (or nearly) of acceptance that Victor had achieved before them.

It is important to try to accept as much of what is happening as the patient does, and to bear in mind that you do not always demonstrate how deeply you care by taking action. Victor's sister took him to the alternative medicine clinic, partly against his wishes, because she was not ready to accept his death and also to show how much she cared. Later on, we all agreed that there were other ways of showing how much she cared. Just being there with him would have been fine.

Things you can do to help

In the final stage, acceptance is the most important factor in deciding what you are able to do and how you are able to support your friend. Accordingly, I'm going to divide this part of the chapter into two sections dealing with issues that arise before acceptance and those after.

Before acceptance

When you *know* that the end is near, sadness and anticipatory grief are natural and have a healing effect. The problem is that very often you *don't* know when the end is close. Wondering whether to help a struggle for life or to encourage acceptance of death is a dilemma for relatives and friends.

To help resolve this, you should attempt to answer two questions: first, what are the medical facts, and second, what choice does your friend wish to make in these circumstances?

The medical facts are not always easy to establish. The situation is most straightforward when the doctor looking after your friend has his trust and respect and there is good communication between them. If the doctor eventually has to say that active treatment against the disease is no longer possible and that the objective now is palliative care (meaning control of symptoms), it will be more easily accepted by all concerned.

Difficulties occur when the patient – or you – have doubts about the inevitability of the patient's dying. These doubts may arise from uncertainty about the doctor concerned ('Does he know enough to be sure there's no hope?' 'Has he heard of Professor Smith in Chicago who's apparently a world expert?'). Other people may put doubts into your mind ('There's this neighbour who had cancer just like Joe's and it was in his liver and the doctors said it was hopeless but he tried treatment X or Y. . .'). When I was ill, for instance, I received dozens of letters from well-meaning people who had seen me on television. They sent me all kinds of miracle cures, the names of faith-healers, magnetic, copper or herbal things to wear or sleep on, and so on.

So, is the illness genuinely terminal, and do you believe your friend's doctor? Or do you keep on trying until the very last instant? I want to make an observation from my medical practice, and then to offer a way of picking a path through this tricky area.

First, there is more suffering caused by desperate struggling than there is by apparently premature acceptance. When I made a television programme about a laetrile clinic in Mexico, I saw many patients who were desperately ill. Some were so ill that they were not even allowed into the clinic but were 'turned round' in the car park. Many had made the long trek from their homes, at considerable expense in time and effort and at moderate financial outlay (the prices were not absurd, but it usually amounted to many thousands of dollars). They were desperate and were concentrating entirely on being cured. They were often angry, intermittently wildly optimistic, very rarely at peace and they spent very little time being close to their spouses or friends.

The attitude of 'I'll go anywhere and I'll try anything' has a price tag. The price is the loss of time to be close to each other, and the loss of that tenderness and sensitivity that might have been allowed to grow.

Hence, in considering 'the medical facts', you are balancing two emotionally laden scenarios. If you accept the medical fact that it is hopeless, you might miss out some (probably very small) chance of a longer life for your friend. If you don't accept it, you have a very high chance of assisting your friend in wasting time and money when time at least, and perhaps money as well, is in short supply.

My suggestion is that if the patient is really in doubt, or if you are in doubt and the patient accepts your view, get a second opinion. Ask another doctor. But if the second opinion is the same as the first, and you have the feeling that you *must* go and get a third, and maybe a fourth, until you hear what you want to hear, then stop and think. If that second opinion agrees with the first, and you *still* feel desperate, you should ask yourself, 'What am I unable to hear?' In fact, constant shopping around is a sign of denial. It's a sign that the patient or you (or both) are not ready to accept what's happening.

There is a story about a famous doctor who was the editor of an extremely prestigious medical journal. Sadly, he developed a tumour for which there was no effective treatment. In his everyday life he read dozens of academic papers on various aspects of medicine. He started calling on experts in the field from all over the world to give him advice. Most of them told him that nothing much could be done for the disease itself and that control of symptoms was the best he could hope for. But he kept on asking more experts and spent more and more time at it. A friend of his recognised what was going on and said, 'James, find a good doctor and do what he recommends.'

Much of a patient's attitude in the final stage depends on trust and the personal bond between doctor and patient. If your friend does trust her doctor and can accept his advice and guidance, then you should support that. It is a valuable resource for her. If that trust is not there, you should discuss the possibility of finding another doctor. The doctor–patient relationship is personal and subjective, and, almost like a marriage, it depends on a matching of the personalities of the participants rather than on any absolute qualities of one or the other. Your friend needs the best match available in the circumstances. A perfect match is rare.

In summary, then, occasionally something apparently miraculous *does* happen as a result of shopping around. Unfortunately, in the great majority of instances, it doesn't, and time, energy and opportunity are lost. Despite the 'How can you give up on him?' cries from well-meaning friends and advisors (who may be unable to accept the patient's death themselves), acceptance of the inevitable and preparation for death is not cowardly or treacherous.

Alternative medicines

As I have said, it is often in this last phase that alternative medicine treatments are discussed. These may materially affect your feelings and your ability to support the patient. Most alternative (that is, unconventional) medicines have a brief vogue and then disappear for ever. Usually they rise in popularity very rapidly over one or two years, ride the crest of a wave for five years or so, then fade.

The hallmark of alternative medicine practitioners is that they do not try very hard to find out whether their treatment actually works against the disease or not. They do not follow their patients up and do not collect information to find out if they're curing 50 per cent, 10 per cent or none at all. They do publicise and they do make claims.

I have met many of them, and all the ones I met were certainly sincere, kind and caring. There may well be charlatans and rogues around, but they are rare and they are not the major part of the problem. The major problem is that most of the alternative medicine practitioners are good with people but not good at treating diseases. They are almost always charismatic, good listeners, and intuitive psychotherapists (all the things which a good doctor ought to be). They are often persecuted or condemned by the conventional authorities, which simply adds to their charm and mystique.

Sadly, they usually lead their patients on (often unintentionally) and then abandon them in a worse state than when they were first seen. Hopes raised, and then dashed, do more damage than hopes never raised at all.

You should therefore think about why the patient – or you – wants to have a try. If it is simply to have a go, and you do it with very little expectation and very little expense (of time or money) then little will be lost. If it becomes a major project with hopes raised high, then do be careful. If there is no miracle cure at the end of it, you are both going to be in a far worse state than you were before you started.

Practically speaking, it's worth checking a few points. How long has the clinic been going? How many patients have undergone this treatment so far? What happened to them? How can you find out what happened – are the results published anywhere in a respected journal? Or is it all hearsay or interviews in magazines? What happens if the treatment doesn't work? Will it do harm? (The answer with alternative medicine is virtually 100 per cent no. Nearly all alternative medicines are harmless.) What does it cost?

These issues, once raised, have to be resolved, which may take a lot of time and discussion. But once they are resolved and the patient is genuinely resigned to the fact of dying, then communication patterns change between you, and this is a time when you can be of major help and support.

After acceptance

At some point, then, whether or not your friend tries alternative medicines, there will be a time when the struggle is over.

To help you communicate at this important stage, I'd like you to try another mental exercise. Imagine that you yourself are in the patient's position. Imagine that you know – today – that you will not be alive in, say, three months. This is not an easy thought to entertain, but try to think now of those things that would reduce your fears and anxieties and make it easier for you to face the end. What sort of things would they be?

In general, two kinds of support would be most valuable: practical support in sorting out the details of your life (what one might call your 'last wishes'), and emotional support in reinforcing the idea that dying doesn't rob your life of meaning, reassurance that you won't be forgotten by the people that you have known and who survive you.

As an example of the first kind of support, think for a moment about yourself even though you're not a patient. Have you made your own will? Every adult should do this: first because it's a good thing for everyone to do anyway, second because it is an effective way to face your own mortality even before you need to, and third because it is a way of bring you closer – in a small but real way – to understanding the viewpoint of someone who is facing death. You will be quite surprised how you feel after you have made out your will: it's a valuable exercise.

Last wishes
When you and the patient are close and you both know that she is going to die, you can help with the details. Help to get the will sorted out. Help to locate important documents. Find out whether the patient wants you to contact anyone (so many people have cousins or old friends that they have not spoken to in the last umpteen years). If the patient has specific views about the last phase of the illness, help with that. Perhaps she would rather be transferred to a hospice or a palliative care unit, or some other place specialising in support of the terminally ill. If they don't know enough about such places, perhaps you could contact a social worker to explain more, or get information from a local hospice.

Quite often the patient wants to die at home. If you think about it yourself, and assuming that you quite like *living* at home, you'd probably want to die there if you could be reasonably comfortable physically. Many families are a bit horrified at first and are very worried about whether they'll be able to cope with the physical and nursing needs. Give it a try and do your best because you will be doing the patient a great service if you can manage it. If, however, it is simply unsupportable and you cannot manage then you should stop and get help. If you do your best and you can't manage it, then you shouldn't feel guilty. Most patients do understand that their family has tried.

An alternative to home or hospital care is admission to a hospice or palliative care unit. Such units are devoted only to the care of patients at the end of life, and usually have staff who are highly trained and experienced in the control of patients' symptoms. Generally, such units have a higher nurse:patient ratio than a general hospital, with fewer doctors. In all of the units that I have visited there has been a high level of support for patient and family with back-up from many areas including social work, chaplaincy, physiotherapy, and so on. Most palliative care units allow – and encourage – patients to spend days out with their families, so that fears of a 'one-way ticket' are not usually justified. Most units also encourage potential patients to visit the unit to get the flavour of the place before they require admission. This is usually a very valuable introduction to the unit and greatly reduces the patient's fear. You should ask the social worker associated with the doctor looking after your friend for details of the local unit. It is often a useful thing for you to visit the unit first and report back to your friend.

Other details may be equally important to the patient at the end of life. Does he have specific ideas about funeral arrangements? About organ donation? About cremation? If so, don't shy away from talking about them. If you say something like, 'Oh, come on, there's no need to talk like that,' you isolate and frustrate the patient.

Often the major block to communication will be the relative or friend, and not the patient. When I was in my first year of medical school, I was asked to pay a social call on a friend of my aunt, a man in his early fifties called Alan. I visited him only twice, but we got on very well. He was good company and a great conversationalist. On the second visit he invited me to his party. He looked very ill and I was a bit confused. He said that he was planning a party for after his death (in other words, a wake) and he'd be glad if I went to it. I was very inexperienced at that stage of my career, and I became very embarrassed. I didn't know what to say. I didn't go to the party after his death, but I've thought about him often and I wish that I had had the equanimity to accept his invitation, and to tell him so. It is not yet a normal social act to arrange a wake for after your death, but it does happen and is usually successful when it does. The great choreographer Bob Fosse recently left a large amount of money in his will for some of his friends to have a last dinner on him. Last wishes like this may give you some pause when they are first suggested, but in helping to celebrate the patient's life they may help him to let go of it.

Sometimes the patient's wishes may appear a little incongruous. Three times in my career I have been involved in looking after patients who wanted to be married within the last few days of their lives. In each case the patient was the man and in each case he had been living with or involved with the woman for many years, but for various reasons they had never got round to getting married. Although it seemed a little odd at first, on all three occasions the marriage took place on the ward in a private room, and was actually a very special occasion. In the third case, some of the relatives expressed doubts about it, but we pointed out that it was the patient's wishes that counted, even though the immediate family were very important to the couple.

'No heroic measures' – the living will

Another area where you can be of real and practical help is in assisting the patient to make her views on treatment clear to the doctors looking after her. Many people nowadays have very specific ideas of what they will or will not consent to in the way of hospital treatment when they have a terminal illness. Most hospitals in the United States and Canada have a policy of asking patients who are terminally ill whether they wish to receive cardiac resuscitation if their heart stops suddenly (a cardiac arrest). Many patients feel quite strongly that they do not wish to be resuscitated (it is always unsuccessful in terminally ill patients anyway), and they do not wish to recover consciousness in an Intensive Care Unit with tubes in their lungs and veins. If your friend has views like that, make sure that the doctors know of them.

One device which has been of enormous value recently is a document called the 'living will'. This is a short document that the patient signs (witnessed by you or another friend or family member) stating that the patient doesn't wish to have heroic measures carried out to prolong life if she becomes incapable of indicating her wishes. The exact legal standing of this document is still being defined in the United States, but it is certainly regarded as evidence of the patient's wishes. In some cases, doctors have been threatened with legal action for assault if they persevere with aggressive treatment in contradiction to a living will. In Britain and Canada, the document does not yet have legal status but it is generally taken very seriously and accepted by the great majority of doctors as a strong indication of what the patient will and will not permit. A typical example of a living will is included in the appendix of this book.

Most doctors – myself included – find a living will very helpful in looking after the patient in hospital. The document clarifies the patient's wishes and removes ambiguity and uncertainty which might otherwise confuse care. If you know this is what your friend wants, then try to get a living will for her, and in the meantime help the patient to make her views known to the doctor.

These, then, are some of the most important practicalities of the final phase. We may now consider the emotional support of someone who has accepted their imminent death.

'You won't be forgotten'

I'd like to return again to the experiences that Ruth went through near the time of Leslie's death.

Shortly before he died, Leslie became very anxious about his son, Michael, who was then less than three years old. As he and Ruth talked about it, Ruth realised that what Leslie was really saying was not 'Please don't let Michael forget me,' but rather 'Please don't forget me yourself.' Once that became clear (to both of them) Ruth was able to talk to Leslie about how she felt about him at that moment and about how she would be able to keep an image of him alive for Michael in the future. I'm sure that Leslie knew that Ruth could and would do that, and her assurances made him feel less anxious.

The story doesn't end there. Ten years later Michael was confirmed, in the same temple in which Leslie had been confirmed himself. Ruth said of Michael's confirmation, 'There was something to do with continuity there. Even though Leslie had died, something was being kept alive, and Michael was aware of it. It was very special.'

In my own case, the time during which it was thought that I might die lasted only a few weeks and, as it happened, it never reached the point when the doctors were *sure* that I would die. Nevertheless, the thing that I most wanted to believe – to know – was that the people closest to me would not forget me, and that we had achieved some things that would count after I had died. Some people gave me that feeling – that there was worth in our relationship – and I still love those people dearly. As a patient once said to me, 'There's one thing you can say about dying – you certainly find out who your friends are.'

If you can talk about the kind of continuity that Ruth showed with Michael, and if you can show the person facing the end of his life that his value doesn't end, then I think you are being a true friend.

I'd encourage you to talk about these things, even though it may seem awkward at first. Tell him that he's not lost to you, and that he's still loved and that you're not the same person that you would have been had you never met him. Tell him, because you may not have the chance later. It'll help.

'I want you to promise . . .'
Sometimes there are demands that you feel you can't meet. There is a social tradition that if a dying person makes a demand of you – a promise or a commitment – you are obliged to honour it, come hell or high water. Failing to honour a death-bed request seems to carry a huge burden of guilt. My favourite example is in the novel *Middlemarch*, where the heroine, Dorothea, is asked by her husband, Mr Casaubon, to promise to complete his life's work, which is a boring and pointless commentary on the Bible. She says she'll think about it and he dies that night – miraculously saving her from a life of scholastic drudgery.

But you might be asked to promise something that under ordinary circumstances you would not immediately agree to. What then? The best way to respond is to think about what you would reply if the patient were *not* dying. Obviously, agreeing to a promise that is totally out of character ('I want you to promise to bring up the children as pickpockets . . .'), or something that contradicts a central principle of yours, is not acceptable to you. In those circumstances, making a false promise will hurt you afterwards. If, however, the promise is something you might ordinarily think about (and we all make promises that we *try* to keep) then you should do so, and not feel unduly guilty if you do not manage to maintain it for the rest of your life. Your life will definitely go on after bereavement; it's *supposed* to. In the same way that you and your friend might have discussed things and changed your views on this matter and that, you're *allowed* to change *after* bereavement. Personally, I think nothing is sadder than a bereaved person living, for instance, in a large and inconvenient house because 'Dad would have wanted it that way'. And when the family plead with Mum to be kinder to herself she says, 'We all have our crosses to bear.' But didn't Dad change his mind about things sometimes, when he was alive? And if he did why should this widow have to live her life by a rule-book written at the time of her bereavement?

'What if I'm not there when he dies?'
One of the questions that causes immense distress to the friend or relative during the last stage of the patient's life is, 'What happens if I'm not there at the moment he dies?' If she is not there when the person dies, then the distress caused to the survivor can be severe and painful, and may last for many years. Why is this?

The answer is complex, and sorting out the various strands that make up this powerful and deep feeling is not easy. But let me reiterate the medical facts about most moments of death. Most people are not conscious at the time of their death, but slip through a period of increasing drowsiness to stupor (as it is called), coma and then death. The timetable is variable, but as a general rule most people are not actually conscious at the last moment of their lives.

Even so, many patients would like someone very close to them to be present at their deaths. Often the relative or friend specifically asks to be called if the patient's condition deteriorates seriously. Despite this, sometimes the person who wants to be there isn't, and feels badly about it afterwards. Sometimes there are good and obvious reasons why the friend can't be there: the medical staff are involved in active resuscitation measures, or the deterioration is very sudden and unexpected, or the friend lives too far away. The reasons are not very important. The point is that it happens quite often and the survivor is frequently overwhelmed with guilt and grief.

It happened to Ruth that way. Leslie was in another city, Chicago, giving a lecture when he felt feverish and took himself to the local teaching hospital (he was on a course of chemotherapy at the time). He had an infection in his blood and by early that afternoon was dangerously ill. Ruth received a message from the hospital; she phoned and asked if she could speak to Leslie. The nurse who answered the phone replied, 'You can't speak to him now – he's dying.'

Ruth says, 'I still can't think about that without reliving the pain. I rushed to the airport to get to Chicago. There was a storm and no flights were leaving. I sat in the airport waiting for three hours. And when I got to Chicago, Leslie had died. The pain was massive – more than anything I'd ever felt before, or since. It was so bad that even now, seventeen years after Leslie died, I can't go back to Chicago without the whole thing, all the pain and all the misery, coming back to me.'

But why is this last moment so important – or rather why do we think it is? Why is it so central that Ruth finds it painful even to talk about the subject nearly twenty years later?

It is due in part to the sense of abandonment ('he died alone') but there is more to it than that. It is almost as if we think that the last moment of life summarises the whole of that life. It feels as if the fact that someone dies alone negates the many years of companionship that may have gone before.

I think this is because we imagine that the person who has died is somehow locked into the state in which they died. If they died alone, say, in 1973, then we tend to have a strange feeling that they're still alone in 1983 and 1993. Each time we remember and think of them, there they are, still alone.

This, of course, isn't true. What is stuck is our *memory* of them, and that is *our* problem. Missing the last moment of life is painful because of the way our memories – the memories of the survivors – are constructed. But years of marriage, friendship and caring are not wiped out by the last few moments, however painful they are to recall later.

Euthanasia

The word 'euthanasia' simply means 'dying well', but there is a great deal of confusion about what it implies. Most authorities recognise two types of euthanasia. There is 'active euthanasia', which means giving the patient a substance that will kill him. This is illegal in every Western country and is regarded legally as murder. There are no legal cases in which a person who has assisted in this act and who has been tried for it has been found not guilty of murder, although sometimes sentences are reduced because of mitigating circumstances. However, no country has yet passed a law allowing active euthanasia. The main problem in drawing up such a law is in preventing abuse, and in devising a system of administering drugs for the purpose of ending someone's life. Although many people wish that there was such a law, at present there is none, and I doubt whether there will be in the foreseeable future. One country, Holland, has a different ethical climate. There, euthanasia is illegal, but it is estimated that every year between 7000 and 10,000 terminally ill patients have their lives ended at their own request by their doctors. Even so, legal reform to accommodate active euthanasia in Holland is thought to be a long way off.

'Passive euthanasia', by contrast, means using normal drugs to keep the patient comfortable even if that usage might shorten the patient's life. This is perfectly legal, and is standard practice on palliative care units where the quality of life is valued. As a matter of fact even though major pain-killers *might*, in theory, shorten a patient's life, usually they don't, and some very detailed research in hospices has shown that patients on narcotic pain-killers live the same length of time as patients at the same stage of illness who are not on narcotic pain-killers.

The use of passive euthanasia is what the living will is all about. It is a humane and considerate way of looking after someone in the last stage of life.

8

Saying Goodbye

So much has been written about grief and bereavement that it is difficult for anyone to see the wood for the trees. In this chapter I shall summarise the central function of grief and mourning, explain how it works, and how sometimes it goes wrong.

I shall divide the subject into three broad areas. First, I'm going to talk about grief itself: what it does, what it is supposed to do for you, the surviving friend or relative, and the stages of grieving. Second, I shall deal with the grief that most people feel before a person dies. Finally, I shall consider the important problem of what happens when grief doesn't do what it's supposed to do, and gets stuck.

The function of grief

Grief is all about letting go and saying goodbye. There are many different theories about precisely what it does, but the theme most often repeated is of the survivor letting go of her attachment to the person who dies, and, by doing that, becoming able to make attachments to other people in the future.

Losing someone close to us hurts a lot. It hurts because of the ties we make with that person. They meet our needs, and we meet their needs. Those ties are what getting close to someone is all about, and generally we let only a few people that close to us. When we lose them, or realise that we might lose them, it is those ties that cause us the pain. Grieving normally reduces the hurt.

If you complete the process of grieving and if, at some point in the future, you are able to be happy and fulfilled and make intimate ties with someone else, that means that grief has achieved what it's supposed to do. The person in whom grief *doesn't* do its job will often end up being unable to invest in anyone else again. (Like Miss Havisham in *Great Expectations* who kept her wedding dress and cake preserved as they were on the day that she was jilted – a perfect example of totally arrested grief!)

Remember: whether you wish it or not, you *are* going to survive the patient's death, and *that should not make you feel guilty*. It may well be that you would give anything to change places with the patient (particularly if the patient is your child) but that is not in your power. You have to face up to two facts, both of which seem awful at the time: your friend is going to die, and you are going to survive. Neither his death nor your survival is your fault.

At various times, you may feel (as many relatives have said to me) that life does not seem to be worth living afterwards. This feeling is common, natural and powerful. It cannot be rubbed out with a few phrases like, 'You'll get over it,' or 'Life must go on.' But an understanding of grief and grieving will help you to remould your life later on, and will allow you to go through the grieving period, without trying to fight it or cut it short, so that you emerge psychologically healthy and are able to achieve the potential of your life after the death of your friend.

The stages of grieving

Grieving is a continuous process. It is continuous just as the transition that the patient makes from being healthy to facing the end of life is continuous. For the sake of convenience, I shall divide grieving into three stages: an initial stage, a middle stage and a resolution stage. There is nothing magic about this description. It is intended to make the continuous process easier to talk about. As with accepting bad news, people in grief go backwards and forwards, as emotions come and go in waves.

The initial stage of grief

The initial phase of grief is often like shock. Bereaved relatives use words like 'numb', 'in shock', and 'dazed' to describe it. This kind of reaction (which is again similar to a patient's reaction to bad news) is partly protective. It's part of the way we assimilate a vast change in our world. We tend to blank out to begin with, then take reality on board in manageable pieces.

The shock is often followed by deep sadness. During the deep sadness, you will probably find that you cry a great deal or feel like crying every time the dead person's name is mentioned or some memory of her crops up. The amount of crying varies tremendously from person to person – there's no 'correct' amount. It also varies from culture to culture. Some cultures encourage, or even demand, a lot of crying; others call for a 'stiff upper lip' attitude. The keys here are the depth of your feeling, and the way you usually express yourself. If you normally express your emotions freely and cry easily, and if you now feel like crying a lot, then that is what you should do. If you have always been a person who finds public (or even private) displays of emotion awkward or embarrassing, then you're not going to change overnight and nor should you.

Some problems are caused by what other people tell you that you should be doing. Quite often, bereaved people are told by their family and friends that they should 'be strong'. What the (well-meaning) friends are actually saying is more like, 'Please don't cry, because it upsets *us* and we can't really handle it.' This is advice you do not have to take, however well meant it is.

Some bereaved people think they should be strong because that is what the person who has died would have wished. Sometimes the person who is dying makes that request specifically: 'Don't cry – you'll need to be strong afterwards.' It is important to remember that crying is *not* the opposite of being strong. You can cry *and* be strong. In fact you'll be stronger more quickly if you acknowledge to yourself, by crying, the depth of your hurt. If you *don't* acknowledge the amount of pain and hurt you feel, you probably won't get strong.

So in this initial phase, pay attention to the pain you are feeling, and express it as you usually would.

In the initial phase of grieving you are quite likely to get physical symptoms. You may feel symptoms of anxiety and distress: nausea, pain in the chest or throat, some difficulty in breathing, general aches and pains and menstrual irregularities in women. Some bereaved persons also develop 'sympathetic' symptoms related to the symptoms experienced by the person who has now died: chest pains if he died of heart disease, changes in bowel habit if it was cancer of the colon, and so on. It is helpful to be aware of these symptoms so that you don't think something new or awful is happening to you. If you develop sympathetic symptoms, then you should be aware that is quite common, and not a sign that you are losing your mind.

The middle stage of grief

The middle stage of grief is the phase during which you begin to realise that life will go on after your bereavement, even though you may not yet see how. It may begin a few weeks after the death, but if you have been through a lot of anticipatory grief it may begin sooner. During this phase, the shock and the numbing begin to fade away, and life begins to adopt some semblance of normality. In practice the 'semblance of normality' often creates problems in itself. Quite often your own friends and supporters, who may have rallied round and become close and attentive to you immediately after your bereavement, now see you beginning to reassemble your life, and they withdraw and begin to return to their own lives. They assume that you're 'going to be fine now'.

You may look all right during this phase, but you may be feeling very far from all right. Grieving relatives and spouses have described this phase to me as 'hollow', 'feeling like a sham', 'feeling like a ghost', 'not being there'. These phrases describe a state in which you carry out the actions of a 'normal' person, but you're not a normal person inside.

Yet again, it's very important for you to realise that this is not uncommon: the feeling of 'not feeling normal' is actually normal *for this stage of your bereavement*. Re-adjusting to living your life without the person you've lost is a huge task and it takes time, and while it's going on your emotions and your behaviour cannot be 100 per cent of what they were before your loss. Research studies show that the middle phase is often the most difficult. They show that six months or so after the bereavement the survivor may well be feeling very low and depressed while his or her friends and relatives have come to assume that the worst is over. If you find that this is happening to you, you should tell your friends how you feel and ask for a bit more support. You may even require professional help from a psychotherapist or grief counsellor if things do not improve with time.

I want to give one example of someone who expected a grieving relative to get over their grief quickly. It's possibly the most extreme example I've come across, but it certainly illustrates the principle.

Deborah, whom I mentioned previously, was initially 'not allowed' to talk about dying by her husband, Harry, who physically obstructed her speech. Harry's father was a physician of the 'old school', who very rarely expressed any emotions. Deborah's parents were the opposite of Harry's. Deborah's mother was a woman with deep emotions and who expressed them readily and sincerely. Both Deborah's parents found Deborah's illness almost impossible to bear. They sat with her all day, crying often and hardly eating. The night Deborah died her parents were absolutely distraught. I accompanied them while they took their leave of her, and sat with them for some time afterwards, while they cried. Harry's father was waiting outside the room, and as I came out, about an hour after Deborah's death, I heard him say to Harry (about Deborah's parents), 'What are they doing in there? Same old performance, eh?'

I was taken aback. Here was a man, himself a physician, who clearly *expected* that parents should be able to get over their grief in less than an hour, that they should be able to stop crying before (quite literally) the body was cold. He was a man who was clearly incapable of expressing or dealing with his own emotions and was visibly uncomfortable with anyone else's. The example of the father certainly explained some of the problems Harry had been having.

I doubt that there are many people who expect grief to be completed in an hour, but nevertheless outsiders may be very uncomfortable (in themselves) with your grief and may wish it to be over so that *their* discomfort is shortened. All you can do, as a grieving person yourself, is to recognise their discomfort and realise that they aren't going to be much support to you at that time. These things vary as time goes on: someone who is uncomfortable one week may be better able to support you the next week if you 'give them a rest'. Furthermore, some people may be able to support you better if you acknowledge their discomfort. You can easily say, for example, 'I know that when I talk about how rotten I feel it makes you feel uncomfortable . . .' and sometimes that makes things easier all round. It cannot do harm.

Being pushed into returning to normality isn't the only problem at this stage. There are often other processes that are very wearing on you. You may start questioning aspects of the past, often to do with your friend's illness: what if you'd made him go to the doctor earlier? What if you'd insisted he try that experimental therapy? What if you hadn't had that argument the week before he died? and so on. This kind of question is common and often painful. It is also unresolvable in the great majority of cases. Of course you cannot simply forget the questions and put them out of your mind. You can't forget them any more than you can forget a toothache or a headache. The questions exist and they may plague you and occupy a lot of your thinking (and perhaps dreaming) time. You have to accept them as a normal part of the grieving process. You have to accept the fact that most survivors go through the same thing; that most of these questions are simply unanswerable; and that the pain and upset that they cause you will fade as the grief itself resolves.

There is also resentment. As in the early phases of your friend's illness, you may experience very strong feelings of anger and resentment, directed against other people who have not lost their spouse, parent, child or friend, as you have, or against healthy people who resemble the person you have lost. After Leslie's death, Ruth found that she felt very strong resentment for many months. She expressed it this way: 'Whenever I went out, I would look at every young man and try to decide whether his life was worth more or less than Leslie's. Did this man have children? Was he educated? Would he contribute to the betterment of society as a whole? This kind of question would often lead me on into a silent rant about the absurdity of a God who could destroy a valuable life in its prime.'

After a time, for most people, grief will resolve. It's the resolution phase of grieving that I'd like to deal with next.

The resolution phase

Not every authority on grieving thinks the same way about the resolution of grief. However, it is reasonable to suggest that the resolution of grief happens when the survivor is able to remember the person who has died with fondness and pleasure, to be able to recall the good moments and to think about them without acute pain and distress, although (perhaps) with some regret. Resolution has something to do with being (in a way) whole again, and living an independent life, even though it is not the *same* life as before the bereavement. Perhaps this definition is again something of a counsel of perfection, and perhaps a very large proportion of people never *completely* resolve their grief, but I think I've given a fair description of the process, and most people do achieve it in large measure.

Of course there are problems during the resolution phase. Some family members and outsiders may feel that in the resolution phase you shouldn't be going out with other people (if it's your spouse who has died) or having fun or starting to live a normal life. 'It's too soon . . .' or 'It's as if he'd never existed', are incredibly painful observations to someone as her grief resolves and she emerges into the real world again.

There's no fixed timetable for resolution. As long as you're moving towards it, it doesn't matter if you achieve it in three months or two years: it's the process that counts. Ruth vividly remembers a remark that revealed other people's attitudes about two months after Leslie had died. Several close members of his family had come to dinner. Later, one of them, a very well-meaning man, took Ruth aside and said, 'Look, you're young and you've got most of your life ahead of you. In four or five years, you may meet someone, and I just want you to know that nobody will blame you.'

Ruth's reaction was: 'Four or five years? What does that mean? Does that mean that if I *don't* appear to be a grieving widow for a full five years, then I didn't love Leslie? Will that be how they measure how much I loved him?'

The whole point is that it's your timetable, not your friends'. You alone know the depth of your feelings and the depth of your grief. Other people's agendas, however well meant, are not what you need.

Anticipatory grief

Anticipatory grief is grief that begins before the patient has died. I've mentioned it several times already. It is important because *most people don't realise that anticipatory grief is normal*. There is a very common feeling that thinking about someone's death before they have died is, in a way, wishing them dead. Actually, this superstition is very well known. In Shakespeare's *King Henry IV*, while the king is dying, his son Hal (Harry) muses about the terrible duties of monarchy that he'll face when his father dies. His father finds him trying on the crown, and, when Harry says that he thought he'd already died, replies, 'Thy wish was father, Harry, to that thought.'

Though I hate to argue with authorities as great as kings (or Shakespeare), I don't think anticipatory grief *is* a thought fathered by a wish to see the person dead. I think it's perfectly normal preparation for a bereavement. We grieve before a death in exactly the same way as we flinch when we anticipate being injured.

However anticipatory grief – however natural – does produce some problems which I'll mention briefly. If the patient *doesn't* die, or doesn't die within the anticipated time, then the relative who has been going through anticipatory grief tends to feel two emotions: first, a sense of guilt for having 'mentally buried' the patient who is still alive; and second, a sense of blaming the patient for having put the friends and family through a false-bereavement. If you experience anticipatory grief you should not feel guilty about it but accept it as natural. However, you should remember that sometimes the final phase of illness can be quite prolonged, and you may end up feeling impatient and then guilty. You can't necessarily prevent these feelings, but being aware of them is helpful.

When grief goes wrong

Thus far, I have dealt only with the way in which normal grief does its work and allows the survivor to reshape her life and to reinvest her emotions in new relationships. But for some people, grief doesn't work out. They get stuck in the middle of grieving. We call grief that goes wrong, and doesn't complete the healing, 'pathological grief'. It can be quite a problem.

One young woman whom I interviewed for our television programme described very clearly her own problems with arrested grief. Her name was Donna and she was twelve when her father died suddenly and unexpectedly. Her mother was deeply shocked and would not allow anyone in the family to talk about him or to cry openly. Instead, she concentrated very hard on getting the whole family, including Donna, back to 'normal'. Donna carried on through school and university and got a job as a personal assistant to an important politician. But lots of little things began to go wrong: she had headaches, suffered from loss of concentration, memory problems, fits of crying, had difficulties with her boyfriends, and so on.

She was referred to an excellent psychotherapist who helped her realise that, because of her mother's well-meaning efforts, she'd never gone through the whole process of grief. So – twelve years after the event – Donna mourned the death of her father, this time with the therapist. The effects were quite dramatic. Within a few weeks, Donna was on top form emotionally, professionally and personally.

I find Donna's example very important. Perhaps the most crucial message to take from her experience is: 'It's never too late.' Even twelve years after the event, with the right supervision, grieving can achieve a great deal.

So how can you tell whether you are going through a slow process of normal grief, or if you're stuck, and experiencing pathological grief? I think the answer is to look for certain signs in yourself to see if you are changing over a period of time. Think about the pain you feel when you remember the person who has died, the feelings you have when her or his name is mentioned unexpectedly, or you meet someone with the same name or visit a place that was special for you. Think about how you're making out with new relationships and friendships. Think about how much time you're spending crying, and how well you sleep at night. Think about your dreams and the feelings you have during those dreams. Think about how often you recall and relive the last moments of your friend's life.

Try to decide if the pain is getting less. Not day by day or week by week, but over a period of months. Are things better today than they were six months ago? (Note that I'm not asking, 'Have you got over all your grief in six months?' What I'm saying is, 'Are you making progress that you can measure in six months?' There's a very important difference.)

If you're not making progress at all, and everything that hurt six months ago still hurts in the same way and *with the same intensity*, and if you are still going over the events of the last few days of your friend's life, then you are stuck, and you should seek professional help, by which I mean psychotherapy. You might wish to try a self-help group first if you're feeling really nervous. Most bereavement groups, if properly put together and led by an experienced counsellor, are good at recognising pathological grief; if they can't help you to move forward they should at least be able to encourage you to seek help and give you the courage to ask.

Another sign of incomplete grieving is a failure to move on, a failure to grow. I've seen it many times in widows of men with dominating personalities – there's a stunting of emotional growth. It's almost as if these widows live their lives by the same rules that their dead husbands set while they were alive, as if life in 1988 had to be lived according to the dictates of a person who died in 1968, for example, and not by the person who survives him. It's worth thinking about seriously. If you find yourself living in a big house 'because Dad would have wanted it that way', or taking on some burden that you'd rather be without because you feel it would be disloyal to do otherwise, think again. And if you find that your day-to-day life is ruled by ghosts and not by you, then it's worth trying to get some help. Grieving properly means being able to live your own life after bereavement, not re-enacting daily an imitation of what went before.

In a book this size I can't possibly mention every aspect of pathological grief, but I hope that with this broad outline you'll have some idea of how you're doing. It's never easy – but gradually it should become less difficult.

9

Spiritual Aspects

Religious beliefs are intensely personal and vary to a great degree between individuals. Some people have a definite and personal image of God, others having a strong but imprecise sensation; while many acknowledge that they don't know whether there is a God, or feel certain that there isn't one. These personal beliefs are often even more central to that person's view of the world than their politics or their taste in food or music are. They may be more comparable to a person's attitude to sex, in that many people may go through most of their lives without discussing their own feelings on the subject of religion with friends or family who are otherwise fairly close to them. This means that discussing religious views may often be a very delicate matter at any time; and it is particularly finely balanced when a person is facing death – an event that challenges religious beliefs almost more than any other.

So many books have been written on the subject of man's relationship to God or his images of God, and so much of that writing is concerned with the mystery of death, that it might seem invidious to summarise the subject here. However, it is important to make the attempt because there are many pragmatic and practical issues raised by religious beliefs which drastically affect the care of someone who is dying. It is these issues that I shall deal with in this chapter. I shall concentrate only on those aspects of religion that cause problems or difficulties for the patient or for the family, or that put obstacles in the way of easy communication between them. I shall not deal specifically with the (quite common) situation in which the patient has a firm and consistent religious belief which sustains and supports him, and which does not conflict with the family or friends' religious views. This is – in every sense of the word – *good* religion, and it needs no comment precisely because it works well for the patient and family.

However, it sometimes happens that religion becomes a stumbling block either for the patient himself, or between the patient and family. It is in these circumstances that outside perspectives can be useful.

I shall concentrate particularly on two easily recognisable scenes, one in which there has been some element of destructive or 'bad' theology, and the other in which there are major religious differences between patient and supporters. However, in order to demonstrate some ways of approaching these problems, I have to address two other theological issues: first, the most commonly asked theological question, 'Dear God, why me?'; and second, the therapeutic value and meaning of prayer to the patient as seen by the friend and supporter.

In preparing this chapter, I have discussed the major issues with several ministers and particularly with John Martin, drawing on his experience as a hospital chaplain, in which capacity he has supported many of my patients. John and I have widely different religious beliefs, and the fact that we work so closely demonstrates that it is not necessary to have the same religious views as another person in order to understand them and talk freely with them – a point that I hope is underlined in this chapter.

Dear God, why me?

We have considered 'Why me?' in earlier chapters, and I have pointed out that 'Why me?' is often not a question but a cry of distress, a plea for help, a pang of guilt, or a mixture of these and other emotions. The difference between 'Why me?' and 'Dear God, why me?' is that the latter is directed specifically at God, and at that particular person's image of God. That question may contain all the anger, rage, despair and frustration that is contained in the secular 'Why me?', but it also addresses questions of faith.

These questions of faith contain three major elements. First, there is a sense of rage against God for allowing this illness to happen. Second, there may be a strong sense of disappointment. The patient may feel that she has observed her personal religion faithfully all her life and is now being abandoned and cheated of the reward she expected. Third, there may be guilt and a sense that God has inflicted this illness as a punishment for wrongdoing in the past.

All these aspects of the question will cause distress if it is assumed that the God in whom the patient believes is the prime mover of the person's life, who is supposed to control all that happens to that person. However, many ministers strongly disagree with this older image of God as a divine puppeteer, who can intervene on the patient's behalf if He wants to. Many of these ministers, particularly those who work with dying patients, believe that the essence of the relationship between a person and God is the way in which God works with the person in the face of vicissitudes and setbacks that are a part of life. In this view of religion, the illness and threat of death are not caused by dereliction, abandonment or punishment on the part of God, but are part of the things that happen in life. Not only are they events that inevitably occur, but also it is *permissible* and even *healthy* to question God when they occur. Furthermore, many ministers uphold the view that this questioning of God – 'Dear God, why me?' – is a way of bringing the person close to an understanding of his own faith.

This central question crops up many times in medical practice. One patient, a man in his late sixties who had been a deeply religious Christian all his life, found himself questioning his faith near the end of his life. In his case, he felt a strong sense of disappointment and abandonment. He didn't feel that his illness was a punishment, nor was he angry; but he was in great distress because of the way he thought that God had let him down. This feeling then made him feel that his personal faith was inadequate, and he blamed himself for not having a strong enough belief to see him through the bad times.

I asked John Martin to see him, and in discussing the central issue later on, John made the following points: 'In the Jewish and Christian faiths, believers accept the fact that people were created free in God's image. They accept that, as free beings, they are not controlled by some sort of divine controller, but rather that they make their own decisions. To suggest that God moves us on a board like some chess player moving his pieces is ridiculous and goes against all good theology that I know. To suggest that God is with us as we struggle in life, that God is part of us as we experience our aches and pains, our joys and our celebrations is good theology and makes perfect sense. The need to blame God for our pain, our loss, our hurt isn't unusual, nor is it nonsensical. The fact of the matter is that good theology would suggest that God is not at the root of all evil, illness, pain and suffering, but that He works with us to combat those things as part of us. Pain and suffering always have been. Unfortunately, they always will be, as well.'

In making this important point – that God is not the *cause* of pain and suffering, but that 'He works with us to combat those things as part of us' – John speaks with the authority of a church minister backed by much theological writing. The pedigree of this view of religion adds to the support it can give to a patient going through a crisis of faith exemplified in 'Dear God, why me?'

To summarise, then, from a theological viewpoint many would accept the notion that it is permissible and healthy for people to question their faith. Feelings of disappointment, rage and guilt as expressed in the phrase, 'Dear God why me?' are neither rare nor abnormal.

The function of prayer

As someone trained in the scientific method, and lacking strong religious convictions of my own, it may seem out of place for me to assess the value of prayer. After all, prayer is not scientific or medical, it is spiritual, mystical and intimate. It is, in essence, the spiritual relationship, between the one who is praying and God, at work. But even though it is so personal and subjective, it still produces an observable effect. Whether or not one has the same religious belief as the patient – or any religious faith at all – it is still possible to see the effect of prayer and to comment on it in the same way that one can observe the effect of counselling, pain-killers, or anti-depressants.

What is clear, even to the outsider, about the mental and spiritual activity that we call prayer, is that it is a transaction between the person who prays and her or his God. Usually, the action of prayer in itself brings relief: the activity of putting into words a description of the current state of things, of emotions, physical sufferings, hopes, disappointments, and so on, is in itself therapeutic. John Martin describes it as 'an appropriate response, a real response to whatever is happening to us at a given point in our lives. If God is our Guide, our Friend, our Helper, then we need to be able to have an open and honest relationship with Him. That relationship can be very helpful and very therapeutic for the person with the illness. It can be one that allows us freedom of expression and freedom of feeling. If life is good it needs to be celebrated, it needs to be expressed and embraced. If life is not so good then that too needs to be recognised in some response to a God that we keep nothing from, a God that we can share with at all levels, painful and positive, helpful and harmful, good and bad.

'The prayer relationship between the believer and his or her God can be very therapeutic. It can be the only way for some people to unload, to express themselves, to get rid of their feelings. Some people are unable to share on that level with another human being, and for them especially that sharing, that relationship with their God becomes very meaningful. Even those people who have a good rapport and good communication with those around them may be unable to reach the same sort of intimacy with another human being that they feel they can reach with their God. No one, a believer will tell you, knows them as well, as deeply, as closely and as personally as their God. This is a time to capitalise on that relationship, to make use of it, to draw help, strength, courage, wholeness and health from it.'

This is a point often missed by those of us who don't pray: prayer is a response to what is going on in life, and is therapeutic, helping the person who prays. But, in addition, many prayers contain requests or pleas, for help, a cure, a miracle, relief. What happens if these requests are not granted, if the disease or the symptoms don't improve? In other words, what happens if it seems that prayers are not being answered? John has, like most hospital chaplains, encountered that question almost every day, and feels that many prayers are requests for miracles. But, he says, 'We know that God is not in the habit of snapping his fingers and making things change. As a matter of fact, that is a very foreign picture of the God that we know and experience in our day-to-day lives. But all things can be brought to God: our concerns, our fears, and our joys. Just as a child would go to a parent with a hurt or a pain, the believer needs to be able to go to God because in the relationship, in the expression of the pain, the hurt or the need, lies the therapeutic ability of the spiritual expression to give ease, and to alleviate suffering. A child knows that the parent can't make the scrape on her or his knee go away but, in going to the parent and in telling the parent what hurts, and in seeking the parent, the child gets comfort in being close to the parent. The act of seeking comfort makes the relationship closer.

Again, this is a point that is overlooked very often. The act of making a request draws the person nearer, whether or not the request is answered, and whether or not it is *expected* to be answered.

Thus far we have been dealing with very positive aspects of religious belief that you, the friend, can encourage and welcome. Let us now move on to more difficult areas – where religion may throw up obstacles and cause suffering rather than relieve it.

Bad theology

'Bad' theology can best be defined as theology that is oppressive, manipulative, destructive and narrow. It is almost always based entirely on concepts of reward and punishment.

I can best illustrate the effects of bad theology by describing a woman called Angela, who was in her early forties when I first met her. She had advanced breast cancer which had spread to her lungs, causing her to have difficulty in breathing. The cancer had initially responded to chemotherapy but after several months it had worsened again, and was now resistant to drugs. As her physical problems worsened she became deeply depressed and virtually incommunicative. After a couple of weeks the depression became so severe that we asked the opinion of a psychiatrist and Angela was admitted to hospital to start anti-depressant therapy. She improved a little and was discharged from hospital, but in the following two weeks I was struck continually by how great her depression was compared to the noticeable, but not severe, physical disabilities. After a few outpatient appointments, I got to know her and her husband, Richard, a little better, and managed to ask her whether she had any thoughts about dying. She cried very hard; when I asked her what her greatest fear about dying was, she said she was unable to tell me. I asked her if she might be able to speak to our hospital chaplain, and she said yes. But over the preceding two weeks it had seemed as if her breathing had become worse, and she now required continuous oxygen. She got into a terrible panic if the mask was removed even for a few seconds, so she was forced to come into hospital again.

John Martin got to know Angela and Richard well. He noted that Angela was more petrified of her illness and her upcoming death than anyone he had ever seen before. After they had spent a long time together, she confided in John that for some time she had been a member of a strong fundamentalist church movement that had originated in the United States. She had been told by members of this church shortly after her original diagnosis of breast cancer that if she went to their church regularly and prayed seriously, God would free her from her illness if he was interested in saving her. If, on the other hand, God did not cure her then this was His will and it was His way of punishing her on earth and preparing her for even greater punishment after death. As her physical condition deteriorated, she was told that what she was going through was nothing compared with what would happen after death, and that this was all part of her punishment for her and her husband having been successful on earth and having a comfortable life-style and home. Her husband, Richard, was not a member of that church and was very distressed at what Angela had been told and now clearly believed, but he had promised not to tell anyone else about her beliefs. She had begged him not to for fear that it would make her punishment worse still. Her children had also heard much of their mother's beliefs. The elder child was very sceptical about Hell and punishment, but the younger son, Robert, was very worried.

John spent a lot of time undoing the harm, and I was able to see the effects of what he said to the family, and to reinforce them. Her breathing symptoms were so bad because she was afraid that each attack of breathlessness was signalling the end of her life and the start of her punishment in Hell. As John removed the threats of dire punishment from her, her symptoms improved noticeably. She spent time out of bed without oxygen, then was able to walk without it, and even go to the smoking lounge and have a cigarette (something I would never encourage in other circumstances!) She began to smile more and laugh, and became closer to Richard (who was also very relieved at what was happening) and her family. We were able to discuss the end of her life with greater calm, and together we all decided that a palliative care unit would be the most suitable place. She died, peacefully, a few weeks later.

I think Angela's story is important because it shows how the effect of bad theology can be so subtle and yet so powerful. Quite often, patients who are under threat in this way have been told not to talk about their fears to other people, so finding out what's going on can be quite tricky. However, if you can spend the time listening, you may find clues as to what is being held back from you. You probably will not be able to undo the effects of bad theology by yourself; it almost always requires someone with authority within the church or other religious organisation.

Differences in belief

Differences in religious belief may sometimes appear to be so fundamental and so divisive that any form of communication is threatened. (The history of so-called holy wars, from the Crusades to modern-day Northern Ireland, are reminders of the power of these forces.) But when we pause for a moment to remind ourselves and each other of what we are trying to do, the differences fade into the background.

With so many different religions in existence, it must be obvious that no single religion has a monopoly in truth and morality, or has all the answers to life's questions. So when a person is facing the end of her life, we as friends and members of the family should be looking at the practical value of that person's religion in her life. It is a complete waste of our time and energy to worry about whether our friend's religion is the path to eternal truth or not. Provided the patient is not labouring under some manipulative and destructive theological guilt, all that we need do is help our friend to use her own religion to help herself. To borrow a well-worn phrase, our attitude should simply be: 'If it works for you, do it.'

In my experience of looking after dying patients, I think that I must have met believers in the majority of the world's religions. So far I have not encountered a problem so severe that it has halted communication. In working closely with members of many different religions, including Christian Churches and both orthodox and reform Judaism, I have called upon their various expert skills when they have been needed. You can do the same. As long as you make the effort to understand as much as you can of your friend's religious beliefs, and try to see how it's helping, then the fact that she uses a different system of religion shouldn't be a problem. All you have to do is to know what religion she has chosen and to respect that choice.

A guide to giving support

In summary, to support the patient in his or her spiritual understanding of death, keep the following points in mind:

1. *Decide if you are close enough to approach the topic.* A person's feelings about their religious beliefs are very personal and intimate. You probably should not open a discussion with the patient about them unless you are close to the patient. Try to gauge how close a friend you are, and what is the usual level of the intimacy you share.

2. *Be sensitive.* Tread delicately.

3. *Try to decide if bad theology is doing harm.* This also requires sensitivity and a readiness to listen without leaping to premature judgements or condemnation. If you cannot decide whether or not the patient is being helped and supported by his beliefs, then . . .

4. *Get help.* You may find a discussion with a chaplain, social worker or psychotherapist helpful. Remember that if you're talking about the patient specifically, you should get the patient's consent to have the conversation, but if you just want general guidelines about good and bad theology you can talk to anyone in your own right.

5. *Honour the patient's choice.* This is no time to try to convert someone to your view of the world, and if the patient's religious beliefs happen to differ from yours, *as long as they work for the patient,* honour and support them.

6. *Don't be afraid to talk about it if the patient wants to.* In exactly the same way that it is helpful to allow the patient to talk about sexual problems that may be on his mind – however awkward or embarrassing it may seem at first – you can help by just being there and listening when your friend wants to talk about his personal religious beliefs.

PART THREE

Practicalities

10

Things Every Caregiver Should Do

One of the most common problems in trying to help a dying person is that the friends and relatives simply don't know where to start. They want to help but don't know what to do first. In the preceding chapters, I have discussed several approaches to dealing with the problems that your friend may encounter at each stage. In this chapter I am going to set out a logical trail that you can follow which will help you to decide where your help is most useful and where you can start. In Chapter 11 I shall go on to offer specific guidelines that deal with your specific relationship to the dying person, but the outline in this chapter is a basic guide applicable to anybody who wants to help.

Checklist for offering help

1. *Make your offer*. You must first find out whether or not your help is wanted. If there are other people involved in support, you should find out whether your help is needed – so make your offer. Your initial offer should be specific, not just 'Let me know if there's anything I can do,' and you should say clearly that you'll check

back to see if there are things you can help with. Obviously if you are the parent of a sick child or the spouse of a patient, you don't ask; but in most other circumstances it is important to know whether you are in the right position to help. Sometimes a distant acquaintance or colleague is *more* welcome than a close relative, so don't pre-judge your usefulness. Do not be upset if the patient does not seem to want your support. Do not take it personally. If you are still keen on helping, see if there are other family members who need assistance. After you have made your initial offer, do not wait to be called, but check back with a few suggestions.

2. *Become informed.* If you are to be useful to your friend, you will need some information about what the medical situation is, but only enough to make sensible plans. You should not become a world expert on the subject. Many helpers are drawn to acquire more and more details which are not necessarily relevant to their friend's situation; sometimes their motive is curiosity, sometimes it is a desire to be in control.

3. *Assess the needs.* This means assessing the needs of the patient and the rest of the family. Naturally, any assessment is going to be full of uncertainties because the future is often unpredictable, but you should try to think about the patient's needs. Who is going to look after her during the day? Can she get from bed to toilet? Can she prepare her own meals? Does she need medications that she cannot take herself? And of the other family members: Are there children who need to be taken to and from school? Is the spouse medically fit or are there things he or she needs? Is the home suitable for the patient's medical condition or are there things that need to be done there? Any list will be long and almost certainly incomplete, but this is how you should start. Check your list by going through a day in the life of your friend and thinking what she will need at each stage.

4. *Decide what you can and want to do.* What are you good at? Can you cook for the patient (taking round pre-cooked frozen meals is almost always welcome)? Can you prepare meals for other family members? Are you handy around the house? Could you put up hand-rails or wheelchair ramps if required? Could you 'house-sit' so that the spouse can visit the patient? Could you take the kids out to the zoo for the day to give the couple some time together? If you aren't good at any of these things, would you be prepared to pay for, say, a cleaner for a half-day a week to help out? Could you get

hold of relevant booklets for the patient? Can you find videos that the patient likes? Does he need the furniture rearranged? (For instance, the patient may need to sleep on the ground floor because he cannot manage stairs.) If so, could you help him to do it? Will there be flowers at home when the patient gets out of hospital?

5. *Start with small practical things.* Look at the list of things you can do and are prepared to do, and start off by offering a few of them. Do not offer all of them – this will overwhelm the patient. Pick some small items that are practical that the patient *might not be able to do for himself easily.* Making a small contract and meeting your target is far better than aiming too high and failing.

6. *Avoid excesses.* Don't give huge gifts that overwhelm and embarrass. Don't buy the patient a new car unless you know specifically that this is wanted and will not cause embarrassment. Most large gifts spring from a sense of guilt on the part of the donor, and create guilt in the recipient. Your offers of help should be modest, and suited to the patient and family.

7. *Listen.* Time is a present you can always give. If you haven't already done so, read Chapter 2 for some guidelines on sensitive listening, and try to spend regular time with your friend. Don't spend two hours once a month (unless you cannot do otherwise); it's better to spend ten or fifteen minutes once a day or every two days if you can. Be reliable and be there for the patient.

8. *Involve other people.* Be fair to yourself and recognise your own limitations. Every helper and supporter wants to do his or her best. You may be tempted to undertake heroic tasks out of a sense of anger and rage against your friend's situation and the injustice of it. But if you make heroic gestures and then fail you will become part of the problem instead of helping with the solution. You owe it to yourself and to your friend to undertake reasonable tasks so that you succeed. This means you should always be realistic about what you can do, and get other people to help with what you can't.

Going through this list in your mind is valuable because it offers a genuinely practical approach to something that is probably unfamiliar to you, and because it quells your own sense of panic and not knowing where to start. The plans you make will certainly change as conditions change, so be prepared to be flexible and learn on the job.

11

Individual Relationships

In this chapter I shall be looking at the ways in which your role as supporter may vary depending on your relationship to the patient. Obviously losing someone is the same in many ways, whether that person is your parent, spouse, child or friend. However, many important emotional and practical differences do exist. My approach in considering each of these relationships is to look first at the overall nature of that relationship during the time of impending loss, then to suggest a scheme or set of guidelines by which you can make a practical plan, and finally to illustrate the specific difficulties in listening to and talking with the patient.

Losing a parent

Some people have described the death of a parent when the children are adult as the 'least unfair' of deaths. It is, after all, in the natural order of things that the older generation should die before their children. Yet for most people the death of a parent is a huge and painful loss and all that much more painful for being under-rated by society at large. I shall spend a little time detailing the many reasons why this loss is so painful for most of us, and then go on to describe some ways in which you can help and support your parent most effectively and at the same time reduce some of your own pain.

For most people, parents are the roof over their lives. It doesn't matter whether they are 'good' or 'bad' parents. The point is that they have always been there, and as their death approaches we realise that there will be a time when they are no longer there for us. This simple fact of life – that our parents are there for us as we grow up – colours our view of the world so pervasively that we can hardly estimate its importance until we face the reality of their dying and the prospect of life without them. A few years ago, I was talking to a writer about my own experiences in facing what many people thought would be the end of my life. The writer said, 'You seemed to take it pretty well. Do you think you would have felt the same if both your parents weren't alive?' Nobody had ever asked me that before, and I had to admit that much of my own attitude to the illness (which was really 'it's not my turn yet') was based on the fact that both my parents are alive and well.

This underlines the vulnerability we feel when we lose our parents. We become the oldest generation; it is our turn next.

So one major cause of the pain (even though it may sound a very selfish one) is the feeling of vulnerability that comes with losing our psychological roof. This vulnerability has little to do with dependence or independence. The practical changes in life-style may be worse or more obvious for a son or daughter who continues to depend heavily on his or her parents in adult life. Yet even the most independent son or daughter will still experience that vulnerability. This feeling may be difficult for other people to understand. You may find that you get short shrift from your friends ('Come on, your mother is nearly eighty.') You need to be aware that this sense of vulnerability is real and not a sign that you are abnormally weak or dependent. It is normal.

A second major cause of pain is the change in your role. Your parents supported you; now you have to support them. This often causes a sense of awkwardness. Even if you are very capable of looking after other dependents, including children or friends, it's often very difficult to do the same for your parents. The role reversal may make itself felt to both you and your parent, and you may be acutely aware of the fact that you are acting in an unfamiliar role towards a very familiar person.

Furthermore, depending on the physical problems from which

your parent is suffering, you may be involved in performing duties that embarrass you both. You might *want* to do these things, and your parent might be very grateful for your doing them, but there will often be embarrassment.

To some extent parental loss is different for sons and daughters. Generalisations are difficult, but daughters tend to have closer bonds with their mothers, and usually suffer a broader and deeper sense of loss when their mother dies. This may be because many daughters maintain very close contact with their mothers. The loss of a parent, friend and role model in one blow can be very severe. Sons may experience some of the same sensations at the death of their fathers, but the impact is often less. This is partly because fathers usually have less to do with bringing up the children, and partly because fathers often instil a sense of independence into their sons at an early age, reducing the intimacy of their relationship later.

However, general rules are not that important. What matters is the closeness and the intimacy that you have with your mother or father, and how you can help and support them in the best possible way. What follows is a guide to working out what your parent's needs are and will be, and how you can meet them. Working through a schedule of decisions like this won't solve all your problems and it certainly won't stop the hurt, but it will give you a grip on what's happening and stop events over-running you completely.

Guide to making plans

1. *Become informed – but don't become a world expert.* Find out what disease or condition your mother or father has, and find out – in broad outline – how it's likely to affect her or him. You probably won't help your parent by reading every textbook and medical journal on the subject. Very often children who do that are acting out of a sense of guilt or a desire to take command of their parent's life. That may not be what the patient wants at all. You need to be informed enough to prepare for what's ahead. It's certainly worth contacting the local self-help groups and information services (for example: cancer societies, Alzheimer's groups, motor neurone disease groups, and so on) and getting the booklets prepared for the public, but if you find yourself spending hours in the medical

library you should ask yourself who you're doing that for and whom it's meant to help.

2. *Try to get a picture of what lies ahead.* This will almost always be vague and uncertain. The doctor looking after your parent will be able to help only a bit because all diseases are variable, and many are immensely variable. Even diseases that are rapidly progressive may end someone's life in between three months and a year (say), a time span that could make large differences to your plans. You have to accept uncertainty, however frustrating and painful it is. What you should do is get some idea of the range of future scenarios. For example, in a particular case, the patient might be fine for many months and then get worse slowly, or she might get worse steadily from now onwards. You also have to remember that the true picture may only emerge with time, and that you may have to wait several months before your parent's doctor can get a more accurate impression of the disease's progress in your parent's individual case. That's hard on all of you, but it's a fact.

3. *Assemble a possible list of needs.* This will be imperfect, but, based on what information you have, try to work out what your parent's needs are likely to be, in physical terms and in social terms. Will he be able to cook for himself? Who will do the house cleaning? Is he able to get in and out of the bath or on to and off the toilet? Is he able to call you if he needs help? Can he remember phone numbers and manage the phone? Can he manage stairs? If not, can a bed be made on the ground floor? There are dozens of questions like this. A good way to check the completeness of your list is to go mentally through a whole day in your parent's life. Imagine his day from the moment of waking up to his going back to bed. At each stage try to imagine what he will need in order to manage. Even then your list may not be very accurate at first, but at least you will be able to make a start. His needs will become clearer as time goes on.

4. *Try to find out what your parent wants.* You should not rush this part of your planning. Nobody coping with the impact of a serious disease can make all their future plans at once. But over a period of time you should find out if your mother or father has strong feelings about whether they want to be looked after at home, whether they would like to move in with you or any other relative, and so on. Your parent may have a very clear idea of what she wants, or it may take time for the picture to emerge. Even though this is very difficult, it's important to find out her wishes. If you

don't even try, but simply go ahead and make plans that you think are appropriate, you run the risk of offending and insulting your parent and ending up in a situation in which you are both unhappy.

5. *Make a list of your resources.* This means making a list of the resources available both to your parent and to you. Is your other parent still alive? If so, how much is he able to do for the ill parent? Who does what in your mother's or father's household at present? What resources are available to them?

Then think about what you have available. How much time and effort can you personally devote to their care, not just this week or month, but if your mother's or father's condition deteriorates over many months. Be realistic: resist the temptation to be a hero or a heroine in the initial planning stage – it'll be worse if you don't meet your goals later.

Try to obtain information about social services: homemaker services, meals-on-wheels, aids to daily living (hand-rails in the bathroom, wheelchair ramps, etc.), domestic cleaning services, and so on.

6. *Make 'what if . . .' plans.* Don't try to map the whole future at once, but take it in bite-sized chunks. Start by working out what you can do if your parent's condition stays approximately the same for a time. Who will do what? Try to match the needs you've thought about with what your parent wants and what you have available. If you have your own family, don't make any of these decisions alone. One of the worst things you can do is to commit your family resources without consulting them. 'You'll come and live with us, Mother – won't she, Joe?' is an invitation to disaster. It creates serious guilt in both your family and your parent and puts you in the centre of a potentially damaging conflict.

7. *Take it a step at a time, and be realistic.* It's better to make small contracts with your parent and meet them reliably than to try to take over all their care and then fail. They will feel abandoned if you don't do what you promised, and you will end up feeling guilty. It's better to make realistic plans and stick to them. Remember also that, as time goes on, the care routines do become quite a burden and the 'glamour' of volunteering to do everything fades quickly.

8. *Accept that all plans should be flexible and may change.* This applies to every plan and at every stage. Your parent may be very keen to

live at her own home when she is discharged from hospital, but when she tries it even with full social services, it doesn't work and she feels miserable. Or she may have decided at a later stage to be admitted to a hospice or a palliative care unit but then not like it when she arrives (although that's rare in practice). You have to be flexible. If you find your plans are changing, it's probably because the situation is changing. It doesn't mean you made the wrong decisions at the start.

9. *Use other people.* Remember that you aren't alone. You don't need to do everything entirely by yourself all the time.

Talking and listening

Children's relationships with their parents are as varied as anything in the human species. They may be close and loving, or the relationship may be a constant cat-and-dog struggle which actually contains a great deal of love, intimacy and dependence (as perfectly illustrated in the film *Terms of Endearment*); or they may be genuinely distant and remote or even deeply antagonistic. Whatever the relationship, as children grow they become independent, and the nature of their reliance on their parents alters. Robin Skynner, an expert family therapist, suggests in his book *Families – And How to Survive Them* that the final stage of growing up into independence is reached when you can be friends with your parents. That means putting aside the conflicts that have developed in the past as you gained your independence, and accepting your parents as they are.

   Accepting one's parents as they really are may not be easy. If for example you have a strong feeling that your parents have never acknowledged your true worth, and have been unappreciative of your talents and support, then you may feel resentful if you now have to look after them. Accepting them as they are means that you have to stop expecting them to change. You have to accept that they are unappreciative and that this is *their* problem, not yours. If after many years you feel that your mother is short-tempered and autocratic, then accepting her means accepting her as short-tempered and autocratic. You should ask yourself, 'How can I help this short-tempered, autocratic and ill woman?' not 'How can I change my behaviour so that this ill woman will finally appreciate my true worth?'

An example of this that I have never forgotten occurred when I was looking after a woman in her late sixties who had very advanced emphysema. She was one of the most demanding patients that I have looked after, and constantly changed her plans about going home, requiring oxygen at home, and so on. Her daughter was an attractive, intelligent and articulate woman who constantly argued with the nurses and medical staff (including me) about her mother's care and needs. After three or four rather difficult exchanges, I arranged an interview with the daughter alone. I told her that her mother's medical condition was serious but was *not* going to result in her death in the next few months and that we all needed to make plans for her long-term care. I told the daughter that I found her mother very demanding and manipulative, and illustrated my point with a few examples. I said plainly 'I can't save your mother's life, because I can't change her or her lungs, but you can save *your* life if you stop hoping she will change.' The daughter's face changed instantly. She understood that even though her mother was constantly criticising her, other people could see that she was a supportive and capable woman. She also realised that her mother was working her like a puppet and that this was what was exhausting her and making her angry. From that moment on, the daughter's response was different. Her mother still grumbled, but her daughter was neither crushed by the grumbles nor prodded into having a fight with the nurses and doctors.

Of course, if you are genuinely and deeply close to your parents then none of this will be necessary, but for those who are distant or who have been emotionally separate from their parents for some time, acceptance is very important. There is no short cut to achieving it, but listening and talking are the means by which you become closer if you have been separated. The key to being supportive, particularly if you have been distant in the past, is to try to understand the emotion that your parent is feeling and to identify it, rather than react to it. That may mean changing the way in which you react to your mother and father and breaking, literally, the habit of a lifetime. But losing your parent is a big change. It calls for different responses. Think, for instance, about what might happen if, some time after receiving the diagnosis, your mother or father says, 'I'm going to die, and I'm just not ready.' You may never have had to deal with this kind of resentment or sadness on the part of your mother or father before, and therefore you may have very little to guide your response. But, using the principles I have outlined in Chapter 2, you might consider some of these options:

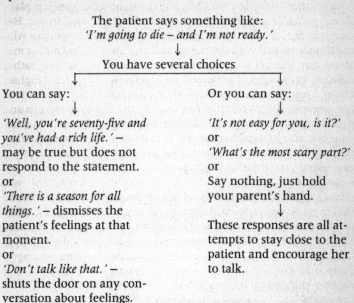

The patient says something like:
'I'm going to die – and I'm not ready.'
↓
You have several choices

You can say:
↓
'Well, you're seventy-five and you've had a rich life.' – may be true but does not respond to the statement.
or
'There is a season for all things.' – dismisses the patient's feelings at that moment.
or
'Don't talk like that.' – shuts the door on any conversation about feelings.

Or you can say:
↓
'It's not easy for you, is it?'
or
'What's the most scary part?'
or
Say nothing, just hold your parent's hand.
↓
These responses are all attempts to stay close to the patient and encourage her to talk.

In summary, then, the impending loss of a parent will usually have a larger emotional impact than you – or your acquaintances – may expect. It may also carry very considerable practical implications for your own life, causing you to lose someone who has supported you in the past but who now requires you to support them. By following the guidelines I have suggested here, you can at least make some inroads that are both logical and practical.

Losing a spouse

Losing a spouse may mean losing a person you've lived with for most of your life, a partner, friend, lover, supporter and co-parent.

Every marriage or relationship has a different mix .of these ingredients and the way a terminal illness affects a marriage varies to a vast extent.

The impact depends, first, on what kind of relationship the partners have been having before the illness: the degree of dependence on each other, the depth of intimacy, the way they share their feelings, the way each understands the role of the other, and so on. The effect of the illness also depends on the age of the partners and their individual attitudes to death and illness, the length of the marriage and whether or not they have encountered major problems before, and how they dealt with them. In general, the marriages that weather the storm best are those in which the couple have good understanding of each other's feelings and each other's role in the marriage, and in which they are used to talking about their feelings and resolving the issues that have come between them previously.

Now, you can't create a new kind of relationship in the face of a major threat, but you can take steps to counteract the way the illness tends to separate you. The key is to be sensitive to the way your partner is feeling and, at the same time, to be aware of what your own feelings are. If you can recognise what is happening to each of you, then you can reduce the feeling of separation that most serious illness produces.

If you haven't already done so, read Chapter 4 to Chapter 7, so that you are aware of the kind of feelings your partner may have, and the ways in which you might react. During the grind of the illness, the main burden of care is probably going to fall on you, and you will become the primary caregiver, the gatekeeper and monitor of other friends and family. Particularly for you, this can be gruelling and exhausting. Of course you want to do it (for most of the time anyway), but it's important to let other people help.

Quite often you will feel angry, resentful or frustrated. The fact that you love your spouse doesn't stop you having those feelings, in fact it makes it more likely. And yet, during this time of maximum stress you are 'supposed' to be totally patient and understanding, infinitely tolerant and endlessly forbearing. In practice, very few people are like that. It would actually be frightening for the sick person if their normal wife or husband suddenly turned into a saint. That is not what supporting a dying person is about. You are not supposed to lose all your own human reations. Nor should you treat your spouse as if she were so fragile that even getting cross with her might kill her. What you can do is to listen more carefully than usual, be aware of her feelings and give her a bit more leeway and a bit more benefit of the doubt when your feelings or needs conflict.

That means striking a balance. On the one hand you should try to avoid full-blooded family arguments caused by your feelings about the illness, on the other hand you shouldn't turn into Florence Nightingale. That balance isn't easy to strike, but it can be done if you behave *like yourself*, slightly emphasising the kinder and more sensitive parts of yourself rather than imitating the saintly behaviour of someone else.

Guide to making plans

1. *Become informed – but don't become a world expert.* It is impossible to stress this point too often. You need enough detailed information to make plans for you and your spouse. Neither of you should – or need to – become a surrogate doctor. If you are spending hours reading medical literature then you are using time that could probably be better spent with your partner.

2. *Think about your relationship to date.* Think about how the two of you have got on with each other in the past. In particular, how clearly defined have your jobs and responsibilities been within the relationship so far? Has one of you always taken over one area of responsibility, or have you shared everything? Has one of you generally been the 'stronger' partner on to whom the other unloads problems? Or have you been able to take it in turns, each supporting the other when the need arose? How have you coped with previous problems: illnesses in the family, job changes, financial problems, and so on? Who usually makes the plans, or do you make them together? If you have children, who has done most of the upbringing? The whole point of thinking like this is to help you to work out what is going to be needed as your partner becomes sicker, and how accustomed you will be to shouldering the whole burden.

3. *Estimate your future needs.* This may require a lot of detailed consideration. Much of it will be uncertain because of the difficulty in predicting the progress of the illness. Even so, try to think about practical things around the house (mobility, access to toilets, ability to manage stairs), and aspects of the medical condition such as how medicines can be given regularly (particularly if injections or other

special treatments are required). Will your spouse be able to use the car? If not, can transport be arranged with other people when necessary? There may be many things that you don't know because you have never needed to discuss them before. If the ill partner is the breadwinner and has been the financial organiser, then you may not know how much money the family needs for running costs or how much you have available. To make a useful plan for the future, you are going to need that kind of information; you and your partner should spend time discussing it.

4. *Get a clear idea of what each of you wants.* For instance, if the prognosis is gloomy, and you may not have much useful 'high-quality' time together, it is very important that you each say what you would like to do. If there are projects or trips that you have been planning together, then you should discuss them. This may be awkward at first because planning for a short-term future involves abandoning hope. If you are both told that the illness is likely to be fatal in less than two years, say, you will go through various reactions including hope. Once you make a firm plan to undertake the trip that you had been promising each other, you have begun accepting the gloomy prognosis. In my experience, many patients carry on working partly because it helps them to deny the illness. Sometimes they regret it later and wish that they had stopped working and taken the trip or had some special time together.

The answer is for you and your spouse to make 'what if . . .' plans. Try to discuss what you each would like to do *if* the doctor's prognosis is correct. This is a less threatening way of finding out what each of you really wants.

5. *List your resources.* Your list should include people, services and money. Think about what each of you can do, and compare it with what you have been doing in the past. Think about who there is to help you. Do either of you have parents who would want to help with the children or come and stay? What about friends or brothers and sisters? Do you have insurance that allows nurse coverage? Are there neighbours who could look after the children when they come home from school until you get back from the hospital? Then you should talk together about finances. Many couples are unaccustomed to having detailed conversations about money because they have never needed to before. However awkward it seems, you should find out how you both stand financially; otherwise sensible planning is impossible.

6. *Plan the future for all members of the family*. Think about each member of the family and discuss plans as they affect each individual, even though it is painful to do. If you have children, planning for their future is of prime importance; however difficult it is to talk about it, you should discuss what to do. Once you have made some overall plans for yourselves and the children, it is often valuable to talk them over with the children. It is important for you to reassure your children that many aspects of their lives will continue uninterrupted. For instance, if you are sure that you will not have to sell the house, move out of town or change their schooling then you should say so and give them the feeling of continuity that they need. It is also important to remember, as you make these plans, that *you do have a future.* Thinking about that and talking about it with your ill spouse will cause both of you pain. You will also feel a sense of guilt because you are thinking about a future which he or she will not share. Do not let that feeling stop you from having these important conversations.

7. *Plan a step at a time and be flexible.* The medical circumstances will change, your resources may change, and your abilities may change. You will not be able to stick to a single plan made at the outset, and the need to change your plans should not worry you.

Problems with sex

Talking about sexual problems that dying people may experience seems to break all the most powerful social taboos at once. It is a subject that everyone – patients, friends, doctors and nurses alike – usually tries to avoid. But it is often of major importance. The sexual urge is a very powerful one for the great majority of people. It is one of the few urges that is powerful enough to be an antidote to pain and misery some of the time. Sex for the seriously ill person can sometimes be the only readily accessible means of escape – even though it is only temporary – from the world of worry and misery that seems to be enclosing him or her. And it is not only a means of escape, it's a means of human contact and a means of achieving intimacy. It is also – because it's a normal activity – something that makes the patient feel like a normal human being, if only for a moment.

However, sex can go wrong when people are ill, and it often does. In fact, specialists in this subject have found that sexual difficulties are almost universal among people who were sexually active at the time they became ill. Non-specialist doctors and nurses have not realised how common the problems are simply because they usually do not ask. Sexual difficulties add a great deal to the burdens of isolation, frustration, guilt and rejection that are already the patient's lot. You can do much to help if you are the patient's sexual partner, or someone they would talk to about sexual problems.

Before we move on to consider what you can do, we should think about the factors that stop or obstruct sexual activity for the patient and you. We can think about the obstacles to sex in two groups: the physical causes, and the emotional or psychological causes, with the understanding that both can occur together.

Among the physical causes, I would include anything that stops a couple from having sex when they both wish to. There are physical obstacles such as a catheter, or surgery to the vagina or penis, injury to the nerves that cause male erection, physical problems with the hips or lower back, and so on. There may be initial problems after bowel surgery if the patient has a colostomy bag. There may be other problems of a more general medical nature, such as pain on movement, nausea, or a headache which is made worse during sexual activity.

Then there are less dramatic – but equally frustrating – physical barriers (which nobody ever talks about) such as being in a hospital. How are a couple supposed to have any form of sexual contact when one of them is an in-patient in a hospital? The answer – according to the unwritten laws governing all hospital in-patients – is that they are not supposed to at all. ('That's not what hospitals are for!' exclaimed one senior nurse when this subject was discussed at a seminar.)

Apart from the physical problems that stop you when you do have the urge, there are many aspects of serious illness that actually switch off the sexual urge itself. These may be affecting the patient, or you as the sexual partner.

Just feeling ill may decrease sex drive. This is because although the sexual urge is quite powerful, biologically it's still something of a luxury, and is apt to be jettisoned at times of medical emergency, particularly in stress-and-strain situations where the adrenaline-producing automatic nervous system is over-active. Similarly, pain anywhere in the body – not just in the genital area – may decrease sexual appetite. Headaches in particular become worse because pressure inside the skull rises during sexual excitement, increasing the pain.

Depression can decrease sex drive very markedly. In fact, this is so significant a sign of depression that psychiatrists note the loss of sexual appetite as an index of the severity of the depression. A lot of other feelings have the same effect: loss of self-confidence and self-esteem, for example, such as may occur after breast surgery or with a colostomy, may reduce the desire for sexual activity. Shame and embarrassment are quite common – even feeling ashamed of being ill and not being in control of everything. These feelings also frequently reduce the patient's sexual confidence and impetus.

Then there are the emotional factors that affect you, the sexual partner. You might find your friend no longer attractive as a result of the illness or some aspect of the treatment. You might be afraid of doing harm – this is quite common after surgery. For example, after the patient has been given detailed instructions about what to do with the operation scar and a list of things they may or may not do, it's quite easy to regard her or his body as 'hospital property'. I well remember one woman asking me if I could get permission for her husband to touch her mastectomy scar many months after the surgery. She was both surprised and relieved when I told her that her body was her property, not the surgeon's.

You might also have your own fears about sex with your friend. You might be afraid that you will hurt him, and you might find it difficult to believe when he says he'd like to try anyway. Wondering whether you're causing pain makes it very difficult to relax. Or you might be afraid that if you are unable to perform sexually in the way you usually do, your partner might sense that and take it as an insult or judgement or rejection. So you might be tempted to make an excuse and avoid the whole issue.

You might also be afraid of catching the disease, particularly true of cancer. With AIDS, of course, such fears are justified and are the whole reason for practising safe sex, but with all other human tumours, you (the unaffected partner), have no reason to worry. This is even true of cancer of the cervix, which is caused by a particular effect of a certain type of virus on the cervix (particularly if acquired early in life); even though the virus is transmitted sexually, you can't 'catch cancer' even though you may be able to transmit the virus.

You might also be feeling angry or resentful. It is very difficult to have sex – which needs a certain level of trust and intimacy – with someone if you are feeling angry at them. In fact, denying the partner sexual gratification is a very common way of showing anger in a relationship.

So these are some of the reasons why sex goes wrong when people are ill. The result is further anger, frustration and guilt. Guilt, which is fairly easily attached to sex at the best of times, is an especially likely outcome. The patient feels guilty for making demands and adding to the burden that the healthy partner is already having to carry alone. The healthy partner feels guilty for denying a seriously ill person something that's clearly so valuable to him or her, and she may later feel guilty if she derives sexual pleasure – or even thinks about it – with other people.

This guilt can be very pervasive. I remember a woman in her late sixties describing to me how she was unable to make love with her husband when he was dying of Hodgkin's disease nearly twenty years previously. The guilt was so severe that she was unable to think of the event without crying, and had had continuous difficulties with sexual and emotional relationships ever since. Many relatives of patients have told me how the illness affected their sexual relationships subsequently when the patient improved physically. Even when the patient recovered sufficiently to regain interest in sex, the healthy spouse's memory of the partner's illness remained for some time afterwards and affected the physical attraction between them.

For all these reasons, then, sexual activity can be halted or difficult. What follows is a guide to approaching this problem.

1. *You have to talk about it.* In my experience, a seriously ill or dying person wants intimacy and human contact from his or her partner *even more than sexual gratification itself.* If you cannot actually manage to join in sex with her, then do not make up an excuse. Do not pretend that you want to but can't for some spurious reason (which adds a further dimension of dishonesty) and do not dodge the issue. You should talk about it and listen. If you feel tenderness and want to be intimate but have a problem in showing those feelings sexually, then you should say so. Very often, an expression of tenderness and concern helps in itself.

Frequently the results of the illness or the treatment change the appearance of the patient so that the partner finds the ill person unattractive. Partners who find themselves repelled by the patient's appearance usually feel very guilty. As a result they often disguise their feelings. This will not help. Feelings of physical repulsion are neither uncommon nor abnormal. You must be honest and sensitive at the same time. You *must* talk about it, and explain that your physical feelings are the way they are, and that your feelings for your partner *as a person* are not affected, nor is the value of your relationship. In these circumstances, as with any other problem with sex, you must be honest.

2. *Be specific about what you can do.* However embarrassing it might be to say so, talk about what you are prepared to do sexually. Sometimes a cuddle or a hug will achieve a great deal. Sometimes gratification just for the partner – masturbation – will help a lot. What you feel able to do depends on you, and on your previous relationship with the patient. But whatever you do, don't just ignore the problem, don't turn over and go to sleep (metaphorically or literally) and hope the problem will go away. It probably will not. Unless you make some effort to deal with the problem, you may inadvertently saddle yourself with a burden of guilt that may last for years and might affect your sexual relationships in the future.

If, as mentioned above, you find that your partner's physical appearance has changed and you are unable to be physically excited by him, you should make it clear that you do not mind gratifying him but are unable to be gratified yourself. That will at least reduce some of the guilt for both of you.

One problem that many couples experience is whether they should continue to sleep in the same bed. Many patients have sleep disturbance caused by pain, coughing or other symptoms and it may be convenient for a healthy partner for the patient to sleep in a separate bed. This is a very important step and may increase the patient's sense of loneliness and isolation. If you are able to talk about sex and intimacy, and are able to plan, for instance, to have sexual contact, and then return to your own bed, you will be able to allay your spouse's sense of rejection.

3. *Ask for privacy.* On a purely practical level, some hospitals and nursing homes are adjusting to the idea that couples really need undisturbed time together, with the unstated understanding that sex is a legitimate use of that time. Again, however embarrassing you may find it, it's worth asking a sympathetic nurse or doctor if a private room can be found, or if undisturbed time can be guaranteed. We've certainly organised that for a few couples on our unit if the patient simply cannot get home even for a night or weekend, and I know of several other units that regard it as reasonable. Be brave – ask.

4. *Get help if you need it.* You can get information about specific medical problems (including, for example, colostomies) from the relevant information groups. There are also resources available (booklets and video material) from professional associations dealing with sexual counselling. You will find some helpful numbers at the end of this book.

Talking and listening

Virtually all the points I have made about communication and support of someone who is dying apply to the impending loss of a spouse. However, when it is a husband or wife that is facing death, the concept of replacement (by the widow or widower remarrying) is a specific subject that merits some thought. Here is an example of the possible options:

The patient says something like:
*'I want you to find someone after
I've died.'*
↓
You have several choices:

You can say:
↓
'Don't talk like that.'
or
'Let's not think about it.'
↓
These responses close the
door on dialogue.

Or you can say:
↓
Nothing, just hold your
spouse's hand – gives a
special moment of contact.
or
'I'll never forget you' –
which is what it's all
about.
↓
This may lead you to show
how what you have had
together will always be a
part of you.

After the bereavement

Starting life again after the loss of your spouse is a daunting prospect. There are many books written specifically on this subject by widows and widowers who have been through the experience and have valuable hints to offer. The one that I mention in 'Recommended reading' is full of practical suggestions for starting over, many of which you may not have thought of but which are straightforward when you come to tackle them. I won't attempt to summarise that material. From what I have already said about the grieving process in Chapter 8, I think I would emphasise the following steps.

1. *Accept the way you feel.* Do not force yourself to be 'strong', for example, but allow yourself to acknowledge and express your emotions in the way you have done in the past.

2. *Assess your needs.* You may now have needs that you have not previously had to consider because they were the province of your partner. You should think about all aspects of your life. Reading one or more of the specialised books on the subject may be most helpful.

3. *List your resources.* There are often more resources available to you than you realise at first. Think of other family members, of friends, social services, financial resources, associations, clubs, local organisations, and so on.

4. *Don't make big decisions rapidly.* You may have spent a long time without close companionship, intimacy and sex, particularly if your spouse's illness was prolonged. Your needs may be many, and the sense of relief that often occurs at the end of a partner's long illness may push you to seek comfort with other partners. There is nothing wrong with this. However, you should not make any long-term decisions too soon. Your sense of balance and perspective are likely to be badly affected and you will probably not be capable of making the best choice for you. As Ruth put it very succinctly, 'For the short-term the message is "date, but don't marry".' The same is true of all major decisions such as moving house away from your circle of friends, and so on.

5. *Get help if you need it.* Have another look at the section on pathological grief in Chapter 8. If you think you are getting stuck in your grieving, seek help.

Losing a brother or sister

Relationships between brothers or sisters are even more varied than marriages. Some siblings are so close ('blood is thicker than water') that they have an intuitive understanding of each other's feelings that appears telepathic to outsiders. Others have a great deal of affection for each other even if they do not meet often. Still others are not even friends and do not like each other, while some are frankly antagonistic and openly competitive. Generalisations are therefore difficult.

However, what siblings have in common – whether they like it or not – is some element of a shared past. Research has shown that if siblings are close in age (less than three years' age difference) they spend, on average, more time in each other's company than either of them do with their parents. Hence, even if they grow apart as they grow older, many siblings have a fund of shared experience which may be closer and more secret than the past they share with their parents.

In addition to representing an element of your past, your sibling also represents your generation. The threat of his or her death, therefore, may make you feel very vulnerable. Depending on your relationship, you may be shattered at the illness afflicting someone close to you, or, if you are totally antagonistic, relieved that it is not happening to you.

There are few general guidelines that can cover all the variations on sibling relationships. However, the following two points are worth bearing in mind:

1. *Use the past.* Whatever your current relationship, the past can be a common bond now. Reminiscence can (if you wish it) bring you closer into a supportive relationship, if you are not in that position already.

2. *Accept the person as he or she is.* Read the section at the beginning of this chapter on parents, to understand the process of acceptance of someone who has been part of your past. If you have been separated, this is a time for mending fences, not settling scores. If you are close then most of the material in this book should help you.

Losing a friend

Friends, like siblings, usually represent our peers – our generation. A friend who is dying means not only the loss of someone near but also warns us that we are mortal too. This intimation of mortality often frightens people away. You may feel that you want to keep distant from your dying friend because otherwise you have to confront the fact that you are not immune from dying yourself. Staying away, then, is often the outward sign of denial on the part of the supporting circle of friends.

Sometimes, friendship reaches levels of intimacy greater than any other relationship. This is more common with women than with men, but as Ruth put it when talking about women's friendships, 'Many of us have friends with whom we exchange things we don't with anybody else. I am not talking about secrets but about a depth of knowing each other and sharing which is, in a way, more intimate than we have with any family member. We see each other or talk to each other every day, and the loss of that kind of friend can be a huge blow.'

As a friend, then, you might be privy to a special part of the patient's personality. You might also be in a better position to help than many of the family members. There are many things that a non-family member can do easily for the patient, because the relationship is based on equality. You can spend time with the spouse of the patient, or relieve the spouse at home so that he or she can spend time with the patient. You can spend time listening to other family members and you may be able to mediate in any squabbles and arguments that commonly arise under these stressful conditions. Very often a close friend has a relationship which is like a combination of spouse, sibling and parent. You can be a very powerful source of support and help.

Young children

There are special problems with young children when dealing with the subject of death. Whether it is, sadly, the death of the child himself or herself, or the death of someone else in the family, the impact, the meaning and the effect are all different and special for the young child. In this section I shall deal first with the problems facing and surrounding a young child who is dying, and second, those problems that arise when a young child faces the death of another family member or close friend.

The dying child

Whenever I think of the sad subject of children and dying, my most vivid image is always of one particular boy, Simon, who was eleven years old when I first met him. He had a tumour in the spinal cord which had caused paralysis of his legs and trunk. He could use his arms, but the tumour (a very rare one) had come back after treatment and it was expected that he would live only a few months. Intellectually, he was very bright and although as a patient he wasn't assigned to me I used to play Scrabble with him (an educational experience for me, since he was better at it). I didn't know how much he knew about the illness, and since I was an outsider, and had no idea of how to approach the subject, I didn't talk to him about the illness at all. But one day, when he'd put down some particularly smart word on the Scrabble board, I asked (more as a joke than anything else), 'How old *are* you, Simon?' He looked straight at me and said, 'I am eleven years, four months and three days old.' I had no idea of how to respond and I couldn't think of anything to say so I just sat there feeling very awkward, and he added, 'And I am dying inch by inch.'

Not every child has such a clear vision of what is happening as Simon did, but it taught me never to underestimate what children comprehend.

The subject itself is colossal. I am going to start by summarising the way in which a child's understanding of the meaning of death varies with age and maturity. Then I shall deal with the reaction of parents to losing a child, and finally offer some guidelines for a practical approach to coping with the huge losses involved.

A child's understanding of death at different ages

Most childen under five years have very little comprehension of the true meaning of dying. This is partly because they do not have a sense of time as adults know it. For a small child, the concept of 'next month' or 'next year' has very little meaning. This means that very young children with serious illnesses are not usually preoccupied with their own death. They are generally much more concerned with whether or not their parents (or other 'fixed' points in their world) are with them or not. Thus, most dying young children think less of themselves and are more frightened about the possibility of their mother or father not being available when needed. In fact, one of the major tasks in a child's early development is learning the idea that people return; allowing Mummy out of sight without anxiety (even for a few minutes) is the sign that a toddler is learning this principle. This means that a young child who is dying will be reassured by having her or his family around, and may not require help in the way that adults know it in coping with the abstract idea of dying.

Children between the ages of six and ten generally become aware that dying means for ever, but still do not have a solidly based view of their own future. Thus, although they are much more concerned with the present than is the toddler, they do not usually spend much time contemplating the future. Instead, they react more strongly to the limitations imposed by the disease (or treatment) and want to know about the illness and why it stops them doing the things they want to do.

Teenagers, on the other hand, are much more likely to resent their shortened life. As a child grows into his teens, he is likely to discover his own talents and have some image of his own potential. He may have decided on a possible career or major hobby and may have discovered that he is good at one particular sport or subject at school. As he begins to understand his own personal potential, so he will regret the loss of what might have been. This can be a tragic and bitter experience both for the young patient and for the family members who support them. It is this realisation of wasted potential, and the bitterness, that often causes seriously ill teenagers to express their emotions in rebellious actions such as failing to take medication or ignoring advice. This is known as 'acting out' and is a common reaction to major life changes at this stage.

After I have described the reactions of the parent, I shall offer a scheme by which you can assess your child's understanding of what is going on, and try to match the support to the child's needs.

Parents' reactions to a dying child

For most parents the possibility of the death of a child is the most terrifying loss they can imagine. The pain that parents suffer is almost impossible to describe. When a parent says something like, 'I wish I could change places and die in place of my child,' there's no doubt in my mind that he or she means it.

There are many powerful emotional elements that combine to make this pain so deep. First, there is the biological bond between parent and child which is an exceptionally strong one. It is one of the major forces that ensure the survival of every species, so the 'animal' instincts pulling the parent towards the threatened child are necessarily strong and deep.

Second, there are the bonds of responsibility. You, as parents, brought the child into the world, so it must be your responsibility if the child is ill or dying. Again, that feeling of responsibility (which brings guilt so quickly) is partly instinctive and biological, which means that it is not easily quelled.

Third, added to the sense of responsibility is the sensation of helplessness. You, as parents, are unable to fix what goes wrong when you've been able to fix so many things before – another major cause of guilt.

Then there are the more social and philosophical elements to the pain. Children are not *meant* to die before their parents. It seems unnatural. However naïve that may sound, many parents have said to me that a dying child challenges their whole view of the way the world works: it's a fundamental insult to their view of the structure of the universe – again, a very deep force. (This force is no less powerful when the child is not young. Parents feel the same even if they are in their seventies and the child in her fifties.)

There is also the strong feeling, which all of us have, that childhood is supposed to be a time of joy and protected pleasure. Illness is supposed to be part of the adult world, something we suffer when we can understand it and cope with it. Illness in childhood is grossly unfair, a brutal assault on an innocent.

All these feelings run very deep. And when a child dies, the desire to find someone to blame is a very strong one. Parents commonly blame each other, and often find themselves in a series of 'if only you had . . .' and 'why didn't you . . .' arguments.

It is very important for all parents in this tragic situation to realise that the risk of divorce after the death of a child is very high. It becomes increasingly easy to hate and blame each other for what has occurred and, later on, equally easy to associate the marriage with the damage and destruction of the child's life. As a result, there is often a strong desire to get away from the whole thing, to start again.

If you are in this position, it is important to try to understand the forces that are tearing at you. If you can recognise that the anger and rage you may be experiencing are neither your fault nor your partner's fault, then perhaps you can limit the damage to your relationship. You may well need help. Talk to each other, of course, but don't hesitate to get help from outside. There are counsellors, therapists and self-help groups of bereaved parents who've been through the experience and know what it is like. There are many people who can help, but none of them will be of value to you if you do not seek their assistance. And you won't go to them if you genuinely believe that it's all your partner's fault (or yours), and if you exhaust yourself in blame, rage and regret.

A guide to making practical plans

1. *Become informed.* As I have mentioned previously, you do need information to make effective plans, but you should not try to become an expert on your child's disease. The sense of outrage and impotence at what is happening often drives parents to accumulate great amounts of information on the assumption that 'there must be something that somebody hasn't thought of'. Sadly, the time spent doing this is time that is being denied to the child, and it often adds desperation to a situation that is already fraught with tension.

2. *Find out what your child understands.* This means you must listen carefully to what the child is saying and the questions your child is asking. Don't assume that all words have the same meaning for the child as they do for you. Check by asking your child what she means. For instance Julie, a six-year-old girl with childhood leukaemia, asked her mother, while I was with them, 'When will I feel better?' The mother was very upset because she thought that the question was about the long-term future. In fact, Julie just wanted to know how long she would have nausea from the chemotherapy (which in her case was successful). By asking Julie what she meant, I was able to give a direct answer. In the same way, if your child asks you about dying, you should find out what she understands before trying to answer in your own terms.

On that subject, you must be prepared to answer the same questions time and time again. Particularly in the case of younger children, this is a part of the way in which they learn things and retain them, and it is also reassuring for the child to hear the same answers to the same questions. It provides an element of consistency in a threatening situation and may actually be comforting for the child, even though it is very hard on you.

3. *Make a list of your resources.* Think about what each of the members of the family can do and are prepared to do. Will the other children take turns in hospital visiting? Can older children or other relatives make meals for younger children or the sick child? If the child is out of hospital, think about the possible ways of spending valuable time together. Or your child might want to spend some time in a 'normal' environment for a child of his or her age. In many parts of the United States and Canada there are holiday camps specifically for children with serious illnesses: Would your child want to spend some time there? What can each of you do as parents in terms of time that is available, special interests (sports, hobbies, computers, and so on)?

It's a good idea to gather your friends round you. They may be somewhat unwilling because of the strong feelings that the death of a child arouses in them. If that's the case, see if they can do some indirect things for you. If your child is in hospital, perhaps you can get your friends to stay at your home while you visit.

4. *Try to work out what is best for your child.* The secret of making the most appropriate plan is not to cram a whole life's worth of experience into the short time that you have available. However tempted you are to try to make sure that your child sees as much of the world as possible and experiences as much as possible, remember that for most children the world consists of family, friends and the neighbourhood. Certainly try to widen the range of your child's experience, but *don't do anything too grandiose.* A few short trips and local visits are better than a massive excursion and upheaval, particularly if the child is physically frail. Sometimes simply staying at home with the family is of greater support and reassurance than a big excursion.

5. *Make plans for the other family members as well.* We shall be dealing with the problems facing other children when a sibling dies in the next section, but it is extremely important not to forget other children when you are making your plans.

6. *Try to keep life as normal as possible.* Everything is changing for your child because of his medical condition. If possible, try to keep the general tenor of your family life on an even keel. This is very hard to achieve, and the tendency to lurch from crisis to crisis is common. But, wherever you can, try to maintain some semblance of normality for your child. Read the usual bedtime stories even if you are in the hospital with your child. Watch the usual television programmes and talk about them together wherever you happen to be. Prepare some of your child's familiar meals (whether at home or in hospital), even if your child has a poor appetite – the routine provides a bit of comfort for you both. Wherever you can, introduce a note of familiarity: decorate the child's bedside table with his own ornaments, buy the usual magazines, get the family's favourite videos, and so on.

Talking and listening

As I have already indicated with the story of Simon at the start of this section, many children have a mature understanding of their plight that exceeds an adult's expectations. We all, as adults, tend to lower the level of the discussion when we are talking about painful subjects with children. This is because we are subconsciously hoping that the child will not understand the situation fully so that we, as adults, are spared the pain of explaining it to him.

While you are talking with and listening to your child, you need to employ all the techniques of sensitive listening that I have detailed in Chapter 2, plus some other important rules.

1. *Pick your moment.* Sometimes there is an emergency and you have to talk immediately, but usually you can pick your moment. Bedtime or a car journey are usually times that are relatively free of distraction, whereas if you interrupt a favourite television programme or game in which your child is engrossed you will not get his full attention and will irritate him.

2. *Remember, the attention span of children is short.* Depending on your child's age and previous abilities, she may only be able to concentrate fully for a short time. Ten minutes is a very long time for small children, and even for teenagers, so it is always better (where possible) to have a few short conversations than one long one. You should also be prepared to have the same conversation

several times, because retention may be limited and the child may like to have the same conversation as reassurance.

3. *Check to make sure how much is getting through.* Do not give long chunks of explanation without asking if the child is understanding it, and try to get her to tell you what she does understand. Do not give a glib phrase and hope that you can get away with it – not even 'One day I'll explain it all,' unless you've already given a fair amount of information and it's not making sense to the child.

I shall give one example of the options available when a child asks a hard question. Many of the things that children ask when they are seriously ill are very painful for you but you should respond with honesty and consistency to avoid making the situation worse.

The patient says something like:
'When am I going to get better?'
↓
You have several choices:

You could say:
'Ask the doctor.'
or
'Wait and see.'
– and lose some of your ability to support your child by 'ducking out' when your help is needed.
↓
Or you could say:
'Soon.'
– then, if he doesn't feel better, he won't trust you.
↓
Or you could say:
'Soon you won't have any more pain.'
– which may not be understandable to a child.

Or you could say:
'If we could make you better, we would.'
– which is truthful and may lead the child to ask:
'Why can't you make me better?'
↓
This allows you to say:
'Sometimes there are things that nobody can fix, no matter how much they would like to.'

Having to hold this kind of dialogue with your child is tough and most parents will not have any experience to guide them. Use other health services to help you if they are available. (Many paediatric units have child psychologists or experienced social workers attached to the unit.)

If there are no other people at hand, you can use books. There are many books specifically written for children at different ages and stages who are facing serious illness. In addition, there are some books (usually written for health professionals, but useful for parents as well) on communicating with children about the subject of death. Books are usually second-best to an experienced helper, but they can be a useful adjunct. A couple of the more useful books are listed in 'Recommended reading'.

After the bereavement

Grief after the loss of a child is always intense and, though it follows the same pattern that I have described in Chapter 8, it is often deep and prolonged. In addition to the material in that chapter, here are some specific points to help stabilise yourself and your family after the death of a child.

1. *Try not to idealise.* The death of a child does mean a vast loss of potential but it is very easy to slip into a habit of idealising him. Expressions such as 'He was always the brightest' or 'I'm sure she would have been a brilliant scientist or writer or musician' may not help you to keep close to the reality of the loss. They may also make surviving siblings feel unwanted and second-rate. So try not to imagine too much from the life that was lost.

2. *Don't cling to objects for too long.* After the death, it's hard to know what to get rid of. Usually the child's toys and clothes provide a form of contact or reminder (they are called 'transitional objects'), but, as grief does its work, you should be able to let go of them. Again, there's no fixed timetable for this, but (as we saw in Chapter 8) if you're still clinging to the child's things and not making progress with your pain and sorrow, then think seriously about getting some help. Perhaps you should try to change the child's room into something neutral – a guest room or a den, perhaps – when you feel able. Avoid making a shrine of it. If you can afford to, replace the most personal items of furniture. Avoid holding on to things because 'this was always Johnny's favourite chair'.

3. *Don't make big decisions quickly*. Just as widows should avoid getting married on the rebound, so you and your partner should not plan your future life too quickly after a massive loss like this. *Don't decide instantly to have another child*. Some couples make this decision quickly, 'to replace the one that's died,' in the hope that it will abolish the pain of their grieving. Sadly, that does not work. No child ever replaces any other child because every individual is an individual. To think otherwise is unfair on the next child, and very hard for you.

4. *Share your grief selectively*. You cannot disguise your grief totally from your partner or from other children if you have them. But to some extent you can control the manner in which you express that grief. With your partner you can explain how you feel in detail, but with the other children it is important to try to express it in terms that they will understand ('I feel sad because Robin has died, but I won't always be sad'). It is most important that you pick your words carefully when you talk about the child who has died. 'He's gone to sleep for ever,' for example, may easily make the surviving children frightened to go to sleep in case they die too.

5. *Don't hesitate to ask for help*. The divorce rate among couples who have lost a child is high. Both of you may be trying to minimise the extent of your loss for the benefit of other children, relatives and each other. This is a natural and appropriate response, but you should not ignore your own deep feelings. Your marriage will not feel the same after the bereavement, but if it does not seem to be getting back together again after a few months, seek help. A divorce or separation is doubly hard for surviving children after a bereavement and with the appropriate help you may be able to avoid it.

A child's response to the death of a parent

In the first part of this section, I shall deal with the child's reaction to a parent suffering from a severe illness and becoming terminally ill. In the second part, I shall discuss the problems facing the child and yourself after the death of the parent.

Children and the parent's illness

During severe illness of a parent, a child's response will to some extent be determined by his ability to understand what is going on. A little child may ask, 'When is Mummy going to get better?' Even if he is told, 'Mummy is never going to get better,' he still may not be able to associate this with his mother not being there. He will be aware that his parent is sick and in pain and is not the way he or she used to be. This may cause an intense reaction, sometimes directed against the sick parent. Fears of abandonment and guilt may well start before the death. If the parent is being looked after at home, the child may feel guilty and unhappy that he cannot make his parent better. He may feel jealous of the amount of time and attention that the healthy parent has to spend looking after the patient. He may also be frightened of the 'new' appearance of his ill parent, be upset by tubes or apparatus, by smells or sights, all of which require explanation to the child in terms that he can understand.

Practical tips

1. *Never make a child do something she does not want to do.* Instead, try to understand what is behind the refusal – it will usually be anxiety or fear. Remember that children tend to express their emotions in actions rather than in words. If they are refusing to visit the hospital, it may be because they are frightened of the hospital, of the illness, or of not knowing what to say. Encourage your child to tell the sick parent about school, friends, and so on. It is usually easy for the child to talk about these things, and reassuring for the ill parent.

2. *Keep visits short for small children.* And try to time the visits so that they coincide with the most comfortable time of day for the patient (just after pain medication has been given, for instance). If the parent is in a stupor or unconscious, allow the child to spend a short time visiting, and reassure him or her that the parent is no longer in pain.

3. *Include and involve your child with activities.* It is useful for your child to make cards for the ill parent, to paint pictures, to write notes – and to see those notes displayed by the bedside. It reminds

the child that he is a valued member of the family. Bring games and things to play with to the hospital so that the patient can have some interaction with the child.

4. *Expect responses and don't panic.* Do not be frightened if your child screams 'I hate Mummy', or 'I never want to see her again', or something similar. The child is experiencing a tremendous sense of loss and outrage at the abandonment. Do not criticise the child but see if you can make her understand that seeing Mummy unwell is hard on all the family. Do not confront the child or force her into behaving well at this stage, just stay close. Remember that a child who shows no response whatever to a very ill parent has probably got a bigger problem than a child who reacts openly.

5. *List your resources.* As at any stage, with any situation, you may need help – and the more support your child has, the better.

6. *Let the school know.* Since the child's behaviour or performance at school may well be affected by the parent's illness, it is important that you let the school know so that they can make reasonable allowance for changes. More importantly, they can let you know of any big changes in behaviour.

7. *Reserve time for the children.* It doesn't need to be much, but it does need to be consistent. You may feel the need to be at the bedside of the sick parent every night and at weekends, but try to arrange for some relief so that you can spend time with your child. You cannot make up for it later. He will need you later, but he also needs you now.

After the death of a parent

For a young child, the death of a parent – particularly the mother – has a major effect. Most children will go through several different and intense emotions, the most important of which are guilt and a sense of abandonment. It is obvious that a child losing a parent will feel abandoned ('Why did Daddy leave me?'), but the origins of guilt may be less obvious. Most parents underestimate how much guilt a young child may experience as a result of an event which so obviously – to the surviving parent – is no fault of the child's.

Children feel guilty because, in their upbringing, they become accustomed to being punished for things that they did not realise would cause problems ('You left your shoes at the bottom of the stairs and I tripped on them'). Hence, when a major event occurs, they search for things *they* might have done wrong that may have caused it. ('Perhaps if I'd tidied my room like she told me, Mum would have got better.') This point is crucial to understanding how a child perceives the loss of a parent, and I shall illustrate a practical approach to this later on in this section.

It is also important to understand that children do not necessarily express their emotions in words. They often express the way they feel by 'acting out'. This means that as parents you should watch for a change in behaviour. This may be the only outward sign of the way your child is feeling. Important changes in behaviour include a sudden change in performance at school, an inability to pay attention, changes in tidiness, bed-wetting, reverting to habits of the past, and so on.

The key to helping your child after a bereavement is to be as constant and consistent as you can. From the child's point of view, a fixed point in her universe has disappeared. Your child will feel a deep sense of insecurity about the surviving parent, and will be wondering whether you are about to disappear too. You should therefore do everything to show your child clearly that you are *not* going to abandon her. If the situation does not improve as time goes on, you should get help.

In the following guidelines, I offer some practical tips which will help you to avoid the most common pitfalls.

A guide to giving support

1. *Be consistent and constant.* You should make special efforts to show that you are not going to disappear from your child's world. Show that you are there for your child, and that you have every intention of staying. Of course you cannot say, 'I'm never going to die,' but you can say, 'I'm not going to die until you're old yourself and have children of your own.' Make small contracts and stick to them. If you say you'll be back at five o'clock, make certain that you are. Do everything to reduce uncertainty for your child, and try never to let her down or go back on a promise. Don't cheat. Don't go out in the evening without telling her, leaving her with a babysitter and hoping she will sleep through. The consequences of being let down by a remaining parent are considerable.

After a bereavement, many children wake in the night and come to sleep in their parent's bed. If you can, let the child snuggle in beside you and then return him to his own bed while he is asleep. In this way he will not feel rejected by you, but will still wake up in his own bed. Many childhood fears return after a bereavement. You may be asked to leave a night-light on, when previously the child was content to sleep without one. Small amounts of regressive behaviour like this (even including occasional bed-wetting), are common and quite normal. Provided there isn't a large or prolonged change in habits, you can accept this as part of the normal response to bereavement.

2. *Make time for your child.* Make it clear that there are times when you are totally available for your child. Even if the child does not take up your offer and, for instance, plays downstairs while you are upstairs, knowing that you are there is important. You should avoid stopping all aspects of your normal life in order to devote yourself entirely to your child, because this adds to the 'abnormality' of your situation. But you should increase your 'special' time, however it is spent.

3. *Find out what's going on.* Watch for big changes in behaviour. Ask your child's teachers at school how she is doing at school subjects and at playing with other children. Often the earliest signs of behavioural changes are at school. If your child's teachers don't know about the parental loss, they may not be looking out for signs of disturbance, and if you do not ask them you will not find out. Ask the parents of other children to let you know if anything very unusual happens – behaviour that is 'way out' for your child. Naturally, you do not want to create an atmosphere of suspicion, so small details should not be overblown, but you do not want to miss something big.

4. *Get help if you need it.* In most households, the death of one parent makes major demands on the surviving parent's time, finances, availability and energy. You simply cannot do everything alone that the two of you did before. So, make a list of your needs and make a list of your resources, and get help to match the first list with the second. You may need simple things, such as babysitters or help with cooking or housework, or you may need special help with the educational and psychological needs of your child. For your child's sake, you must not be frightened of asking.

4. *Keep your roles clear.* After a parental loss, a child may try to 'become' the lost parent in order to fill the gap. A daughter may want very much to 'become' the mother who has died, and to run

the home. This occurs quite frequently. In some respects it's good in the sense that the daughter feels needed and wanted. It may reduce the impact of the loss. But it can endanger the normal growth and development of the child. If a daughter of, say, nine or ten years old becomes the housewife, replacing the mother and looking after other children, her own growth and development through her teens can be difficult. A further problem will arise if, at a later date, you wish to remarry or introduce another adult into the family. Then you will be replacing and apparently rejecting the child in her 'new' role.

If your child does attempt to take the place of the parent who has died, however valuable and useful it seems in the short term, you should talk it over with someone experienced in child guidance and therapy.

Talking and listening

1. *Try to deal with guilt before it becomes a problem.* Reinforce as often as you can the fact that the parent who died did not *want* to leave the family. You need to stress the fact that some things happen that are *nobody*'s fault and which cannot be avoided or fixed by adults, no matter how willing they are or how capable they have been of fixing other things. When Leslie died, Ruth achieved this by drawing a special book for her young son Michael. It showed a family of birds in which the father bird had been killed accidentally, and the mother bird and baby bird lived alone in the nest. This became Michael's favourite book and he would read it to his toys, explaining death to them. It was very hard and sad for adult relatives to hear him do this and to maintain a smiling and interested face while he did, but it removed all elements of guilt, allowing Michael a very early acceptance of what had happened. Depending on your child's age, there are several books available commercially which deal with the loss of a parent.

2. *Don't shy away from reminiscence.* The parent who has died was an important part of your child's life and it is foolish and dangerous to pretend otherwise. One patient of mine, Frances, became a widow in her early thirties. She removed everything from the house that related to her husband, who had died suddenly. His name was not mentioned, there was no grieving within the family, and life simply started up instantly without him. Although this allowed Frances to

get on with her own life almost immediately, it was extremely hard on her children who had no opportunity to grieve, and nobody who would allow them to talk about their father. This caused a great deal of strain within the family.

You should not, therefore, shy away from reminiscence with other family members. Keep the photos (and videos or films if you have them), particularly if they show an affectionate or happy scene of the child with the parent who has died. If you find the pictures too painful to look at yourself, put them in an album so that your child can look at them. Certainly it is sad to recall good times when they are gone, but it is far better to do that – and to accept it – than to pretend you never had them.

3. *Share your grief appropriately.* You cannot totally conceal your own grief from your child, and you should not try. Trying to hide your true feelings will simply make your child feel even more excluded and rejected. On the other hand, the *way* you express your grief is quite important. Use language that the child can understand, and be specific about what it means ('Sometimes I feel sad when I think about Daddy and I miss him, but I love you and I'll feel better soon.') You should shield your child from the undiluted force of your own despair. Don't say anything like, 'I feel so terrible that I don't know how I'm going to cope.'

In talking about your own feelings you should also be aware that your child might experience anger. Usually the anger is directed at the parent who has died, and the child is often angry at having been abandoned. This can be made worse if you or anyone else tries to reduce the child's pain by painting a very bright picture of an after-life, such as 'Mummy's gone to a lovely place where she's very happy'. You should take care to avoid making your child's sense of being abandoned even more intense.

A child's response to the death of a sibling

The death of a brother or sister is also devastating, particularly if the siblings were close in age and spent a lot of time together. The surviving child will almost certainly feel very lonely and very confused. She may spend a lot of energy trying to work out why the sibling that died was 'chosen' to die, and not her. This can be made worse by idealising or glorifying the child who has died – even with the best intentions ('Your brother Bobby was always so good, and so cheerful.') The surviving sibling may feel very guilty that she is still alive when the 'good' brother or sister has died, and may develop low self-esteem. As with the death of a parent, the child may also think and talk about joining the child who has died. This is not common, but if it does happen you should get some help.

In summary then, what I'm saying about children and dying is that there are some specific factors that you need to be aware of. Try to talk to children at the right level – which means talking, listening and asking – and remember that they may go through a whole slew of different emotions as they try to make sense of the idea of dying. And, finally, don't hesitate to get some help. A death in the family is devastating for you and even more so for the children. Getting help now when the problems are beginning is a lot easier than leaving it until later.

12

AIDS and dementing diseases

In this chapter I shall concentrate on two situations in which support of the dying person is particularly difficult: when the patient has either AIDS, or a disease involving loss of mental capacity.

In practice, the 'specialness' of the disease is not very important. All the processes described in previous chapters still go on, and what works to improve communication between patient and relative will still work whether the patient has cancer of the breast, motor neurone disease or AIDS.

However, there are certain social factors that operate (particularly with a disease such as AIDS) that make the supporter's task more difficult, and in this chapter I'm going to focus on these.

AIDS

You probably don't need reminding that AIDS is a disease of the immune system caused by a virus. The virus can be transmitted sexually in body fluids, by contaminated needles used by addicts, by blood transfusions before screening was routine, and by the mother to the foetus inside the womb. The virus itself is rather weak and easily killed outside the body. It cannot be transmitted by casual contact or by contact with objects that have been handled by AIDS patients. Once infected with the virus, the patient may or may not develop the disease itself. If the disease does develop, it makes the patient prone to many different kinds of infection, including certain kinds of pneumonia that are rare in the unaffected population. The virus also makes the patients prone to certain kinds of tumour, including a cancer of the skin called Kaposi's sarcoma, and a cancer of the lymph glands called lymphoma (which is a fairly common tumour anyway – most patients with lymphoma do not have AIDS). The most important thing to remember – and it is hard to hold on to facts when there is so much hysteria and over-reaction – is that you can't catch AIDS by casual contact with a patient. If you have a friend with AIDS you won't catch it by visiting him or her.

But because the homosexual population is the most readily identifiable group at high risk of developing AIDS, many social pressures are added to the burden of the AIDS patient and friends. Fear and distrust of homosexuals – a social phenomenon sometimes called homophobia – is fairly deep-rooted in many cultures. Like all fears of a group that can be identified fairly easily, it is an easy fear to whip up and exploit. In that respect, homophobia is similar to racism or anti-Semitism. It is not difficult to convince some part of the population that they are Us, and that another group is a distinct Them. That has always been a very easy and quick way to raise a great deal of distrust and fear. If you can show that They have a disease because of something They do, and that They are therefore a threat to Us, you can fuel the fire with self-justified rage. This is the reasoning that leads to naming AIDS the 'gay plague' and suggests that it is a visitation by God. It is interesting that it is so much more difficult to identify, say, smokers as a 'Them' despite the fact that They (smokers) die in much larger numbers than do AIDS victims, and that They are a threat to Us (I mean us non-smokers) in the form of passive smoking. I suppose the difference between smoking habits and sexual practices lies in the social taboos and embarrassments surrounding sex, so that there is a ready-made source of fear and ignorance which is so much easier to ignite in the case of AIDS victims.

Thus a person suffering from AIDS finds himself or herself on the other side of the fence from Us. Many AIDS patients are denied the common social charity and sympathy that they would get if they were suffering from, say, multiple sclerosis or arthritis. It is almost as if the suffering of an AIDS patient isn't *really* suffering at all because 'he brought it on himself'. This is an attitude that nobody would dream of applying to a person with lung cancer from smoking or a teenager paralysed from the neck down because he was driving while intoxicated.

In some respects, AIDS is occupying the same position in our society as syphilis did a century ago. Then, syphilis was the vengeful killer punishing Those who had Strayed – or even their children. (The Ibsen plays *Ghosts* and *A Doll's House* both have characters struck down by syphilis as a judgement on them.) The disease was invested with an aura of mysticism and Divine Retribution. Now that we know it is caused by a bacterium and is (in the vast majority of cases) curable by antibiotics, it is merely a serious infection. Exactly the same was true of tuberculosis until the 1940s. It may be that in years to come AIDS will be controlled by safe sexual practices and by vaccination, perhaps even by treatment, in which case it, too, will lose most of its mystical significance.

Until then, AIDS is a disease that puts its victims into a special category, one that some people think should prevent them from getting the kind of human and humane treatment any other sick person could claim as a right. As a result, AIDS patients are not only facing the social taboos associated with death and dying, but also the other taboos to do with homosexuality and 'immorality', which adds to their already heavy burden of facing death at a young age.

Their families and friends suffer from the same social stigmata. Sometimes the diagnosis of AIDS will lead parents to realise for the first time that their son is homosexual, so that they have to confront imminent bereavement, suffering and shame in one devastating blow.

And on top of all that, there are some religious aspects that make the burden even heavier.

Religion and AIDS

In a television film I made in 1983 about people's attitudes to AIDS, we used some film of a leader of a fundamentalist church speaking (or, rather, shouting) about AIDS. He was apoplectic with rage, and spoke of AIDS as the gay plague brought down by God to punish homosexuals for their sins. My immediate reaction to watching that preacher rant and rave was, 'Would Jesus have said these things?'

The issue is an important one, because many AIDS victims are members of Churches and have strong religious convictions. When they are condemned by their own Church, it causes deep pain and cuts them off from yet another source of comfort and sustenance. The fundamentalists say that homosexuality is recognised as a sin (which applies in many branches of the Christian faith, including Roman Catholicism), and therefore anyone who practises homosexuality is, by definition, beyond the boundary of the Church and justly deserves the retribution of God.

To me, the spectacle of the fundamentalist minister raging against AIDS was a sickening one. Here, I thought, was a Christian who had wandered a long way from the teaching of Christ. The principles of Christ's teachings are accessible to anyone, whatever his religious beliefs, and are easy to understand. Jesus made a particular point of working among the people that the society of the time rejected. He went to the lepers (who were even more feared and rejected at that time than AIDS victims are today); he blessed prostitutes (including Mary Magdalen); and protected what we would now call the human rights of adulterers (about one of whom he said, 'He that is without sin among you, let him first cast a stone.') His central teaching was concerned with forgiveness, tolerance and charity. The only people with whom he became angry were the money-lenders in the Temple.

Condemnation of people who are already suffering was no part of Christ's doctrine.

In fact, as I learned when John Martin and I were discussing this issue, Christ had a particular point to make in the parable of the Good Samaritan. John pointed out to me that in Biblical times Samaritans had a very unattractive reputation. 'They were regarded as the scum of the earth. They had about the same social standing as gypsies did under the Nazis. They were thought of as untrustworthy, unsavoury, dishonest and dirty. Christ chose a Samaritan as the central figure of that parable because he wanted to say that it is a man's behaviour that makes him a neighbour, not his social standing or the stratum of society from which he comes. If Jesus were on earth today, he might easily have taken an AIDS carrier as the central figure of that parable: and He might have shown those people who are so ready to condemn AIDS carriers that AIDS carriers – like preachers, like doctors, like all human beings – are to be recognised by their behaviour, their love and their charity. And not by the results of their blood tests.'

What we all need to do for AIDS patients is to *undo* the damage that bigotry, fear, ignorance, prejudice and hate have already done. If you are helping and supporting a person with AIDS, and are experiencing difficulty communicating easily with him, you should concentrate hard on treating that person as you would any other person with a similarly lethal disease. If you can ask yourself, 'How would I behave if this person were dying of something other than AIDS?' then you can at least partially counteract the social pressures acting on you.

Diseases involving loss of mental function

Another medical problem that seems to set its victims apart from the rest of society is loss of mental function, or 'dementia'. Loss of mental ability can accompany many diseases of the brain and nervous system, including Alzheimer's disease, Huntingdon's chorea and advanced stages of multiple sclerosis. In such situations there are special difficulties. The person who was previously loved and appreciated by friends and family 'disappears' and is replaced by a forgetful, irritable, unintelligible ghost, who *looks* like the person everyone knew. This is hard on the family. They get angry and frustrated (which is to be expected, and is the normal reaction) and then feel guilty about their anger. If this happens to you, you may find yourself trying to compensate for your imagined negligence by setting yourself greater targets of help and support which may then increase your feelings of guilt further.

There may be two different forces acting in your mind. On the one hand, if the dementia is advanced, you know that this human being is irrational and disorientated, that it is no use trying to reason with him, and that he may not remember what you say. On the other hand, the physical appearance of the person is still your father or mother or friend, and that appearance still recalls your past emotional investment and gets reflex responses from you.

If you have not already done so, read the section in Chapter 11 on 'Losing a Parent', which will give you a logical structure to assessing and planning for a person's needs. In addition to the points I have made there, I would stress the additional demands made on the supporter when the patient is not rational. The supporter's task is difficult because it calls for as much tolerance and even-temperedness as you can manage, but at the same time you have to remind yourself that the person you knew is not there. It is as if you need to detach yourself emotionally enough to protect yourself from desperate frustration, while simultaneously keeping close enough in to look after your friend physically. This is hard and wearying, and it may bring you to the point at which you think you simply cannot copy. If that happens, it is very important that you think hard about the other resources available to help you to support the patient (other members of the family, other social services) and also other resources that may be of value *to you*. Many self-help groups are of value in this context because they provide a forum for the supporter to ventilate the frustrations of caring for a person with dementia. They may not alter the physical and psychological pressures on you, but by allowing you to blow off steam, they may reduce their impact on your own life.

A critical point in the course of a person's dementing illness is the point at which she can no longer be looked after at home. There may well be a stage at which you and your family can no longer bear the strain of looking after a demented relative. At that point, it would be quite normal to find an institution for her. The problem is that doing this almost always makes the family feel even more guilty. Because the patient is being institutionalised not because of some identifiable medical condition like paralysis or pain, but because the family 'can't take it any more', the family members may feel they have failed. In practice, this is not so. Families consist of human beings and there is a limit to what any family can tolerate without asking for help. If it is necessary, in order to save the mental health of your family, that the person with dementia be looked after elsewhere, then it is necessary. This does not imply that you have failed as a son or daughter. You can only do your best.

In summary, looking at the 'special' cases of AIDS and illnesses that cause dementia, it must be stressed that personal losses have more common factors than differences. Every *person* is different and there are special factors operating in each case, but the mechanisms by which friends and the family recognise what is going on, and the ways in which you can help, are remarkably similar.

13

Talking with Health Professionals

The most common cause of patients or relatives being dissatisfied with the care provided is a gap in communication. While some complaints about the standard of doctors' communication are justified, on some occasions it is the fault of the patient or relative in not making their wishes clearly known. In most cases both parties must share some blame. Communications do sometimes just get off on the wrong foot. In this chapter I am going to offer a simple check-list that you can go through in order to get the maximum out of your discussions with your friend's doctors or nurses. It may not turn a disagreement into peace and harmony but at least it will ensure that you get your part right.

Of course, doctors and nurses are only part of the team, but they are usually the gatekeepers and you need to get them to understand your friend's needs so that the right auxiliary services can be called in. For instance, there are (to name a few) visiting nurses, social workers, counsellors, chaplains, occupational therapists, physiotherapists, psychotherapists, psychiatrists, home care teams and palliative care unit teams. In situations where the right help isn't reaching the patient, the most common problem is a communication gap. Either the doctors looking after the overall care of the patient aren't aware of what the needs are, or the patient and friends aren't aware of what they can ask for.

Here is a simple scheme that you can follow to maximise your chance of communicating effectively:

1. *Decide what kind of conversation you want to have.* Think clearly about what you want to say. There are really only four major types of conversation.

(a) You want information from the doctor about the disease, treatment or prognosis, either for your benefit or to clarify matters for the patient.
(b) You want to give information about the patient's state or needs to the doctor or nurse.
(c) You want to request additional services, support or treatment for the patient.
(d) You want support for yourself – to unburden yourself or get help.

Decide before you start which – or all – of these elements are on your agenda. It may be helpful to write them down for yourself (though it may be advisable not to have the list in front of you when you talk: some doctors react badly to written lists unless they have previously invited you to draw one up).

2. *Determine the urgency of the conversation.* And tell the doctor, nurse or secretary whether you need to talk urgently or not. Sudden and dramatic changes in your friend's condition are urgent and you should call the nurse (in hospital) or emergency services, or (if the situation does not quite qualify as an emergency) the family doctor. But for all other conversations, when you are making an appointment to talk with the doctor give some indication of the priority. If your normal line of communication to the doctor is through a nurse, write down your name and number on a piece of paper. One of the most common causes of communication gap is a message that someone forgot to deliver because they were busy.

You should also give some indication of how long you think you will need. A conversation of fifteen or twenty minutes can accomplish a great deal and would not be an unreasonable demand.

3. *Consider talking on the phone.* Many doctors are better at talking on the phone (it may feel less threatening to them), particularly if you have already met face to face. Consider whether what you have to say or ask can be accomplished over the phone, and if so try that first. It may be quicker and less fussy for both of you.

4. *Be specific.* Try not to meander (although this happens often when people are nervous or under pressure of time). Come to the point as quickly as you can and, bearing in mind the four kinds of conversation mentioned above, try to wrap each point in a way that calls for a specific response from the doctor or nurse.

5. *Expect some uncertainty.* Sadly, many questions – and often the most important ones – cannot be answered easily. In particular, questions about the future, no matter how well you pose them, and how willing the doctor is to answer them, are often unanswerable. The doctor's responses may lack useful precision. Usually he is not hedging, it is simply the way things are. You should be prepared to accept uncertainty, however painful it is.

6. *Get updated.* Put in a quick call to the ward on days when you cannot visit. Getting news in small daily pieces is preferable to visiting after a few days and finding the situation has changed (with all the alarm and anxiety that may cause you).

7. *If you are dissatisfied, pause.* Recall what was mentioned in Chapter 5 about anger and blame. If you think the doctors or nurses are providing unsatisfactory care, ask yourself whether you might actually be angry at the disease. Blaming the bearer for the bad news is a common reaction. Make sure that you are not in the grip of that reaction when you complain. Give yourself a little time to think about that before you take action. If you are sure that the care is unsatisfactory, tell the nurse in as cool and factual a manner as you can. If you still do not get satisfaction, speak to the doctor and then consider (after a further period of time) speaking to the hospital ombudsman, patient representative, patient advocate or administrator. Do not do this unless you really have to. It introduces an atmosphere of adversarial conflict into patient care which makes even simple communications later on more complex.

7. *Tick what's right.* Doctors and nurses enter the health professions because they want to help people, and they like being told if they have done a good job. An appreciative note (if they deserve it) makes their day. It also reinforces good supportive behaviour on the part of the doctor or nurse for the next patient. Even doctors are human.

Appendix A

The living will

There are many versions in circulation at present. The usual format includes some variation of the following (supplied by Dying with Dignity, Toronto, Canada):

To my family, my physicians, my lawyer, and all others whom it may concern:

If the time comes when I can no longer take part in decisions for my own future, let this statement stand as an expression of my wishes and directions, while I am still of sound mind.

If at such a time the situation should arise in which there is no reasonable expectation of my recovery from extreme physical or mental disability, I direct that I be allowed to die and not be kept alive by medications, artificial means or 'heroic measures'. I do, however, ask that medication be mercifully administered to me to alleviate suffering even though this may shorten my remaining life.

This statement is made after careful consideration and is in accordance with my strong convictions and beliefs. I want the wishes and directions here expressed carried out to the extent permitted by law. Insofar as they are not legally enforceable, I hope that those to whom this Will is addressed will regard themselves as morally bound by these provisions.

Signed...................... Date ....
Witness ....
Witness ....
Copies of this request have been given to ....
....

Appendix B

Supporting organisations

Self-help groups

There are many self-help groups throughout the United Kingdom, composed of people working together to help others cope with the same illnesses or problems that they themselves have experienced first hand, be it specific diseases, bereavement, or widowhood.
For information on self-help groups, contact:

National Self-Help Support Centre
26 Bedford Square
London
WC1B 3HU

Other organisations

British Voluntary Euthanasia Society
13 Prince of Wales Terrace
London W8 5PG
01-937-7770

Hospice Information Service
St Christopher's Hospice
51–59 Lawrie Park Rd
London SE26 6DZ
01-778-9252

The Hospice Information Service publishes a directory of the hospices throughout the UK. It also lists all other services available to help patients with cancer or amyotrophic lateral sclerosis.

Reverend Francis O'Leary
Jospice International
St Joseph's Hospice Association
Ince Road
Thorton
Liverpool L23 4UE

Hospices for the terminally ill and those ill but treatable with no one to care for them in Liverpool, England; Pakistan; Colombia; Peru; Ecuador; Honduras; Guatemala.

Cancer Relief Macmillan Fund
Anchor House
15–19 Britten Street
London SW3 3TZ
01-351-7811

Provides support for all cancer patients.

Marie Curie Cancercare
28 Belgrave Square
London SW1X 8QG

Cancerlink
46 Pentonville Road
London
N1 9HF
01-833-2451

Cancerlink is a national organisation offering two services: information and support about all aspects of cancer for patients and their families and friends, as well as a group support service linking up self-help groups throughout Britain.

BACUP
British Association of Cancer United Patients
121–123 Charterhouse Street
London EC1M 6AA
01-608-1661

BACUP offers a national cancer information service with oncology nurses as well as a counselling service with volunteers who provide support for all aspects of cancer and bereavement and can direct callers to a wide variety of community resources.

World Federation of Right to Die Societies
c/o Association pour le droit de mourir dans la dignité (ADMD)
103 rue la Fayette
75010 Paris, France

The Terrence Higgins Trust
BM AIDS
London WC1N 3XX
01-242 1010

Frontliners
BM AIDS
London WC1N 3XX
01-242 1010

Mildmay Mission Hospital (Hospice)
Hackney Road
London E2 7NA
01-379 2331

Recommended Reading

Books with specific advice

Carrol, David. *Living with Dying*. McGraw Hill, 1985.

Grollman, Earl. *Explaining Death to Children*. Beacon Press, 1967.

Myers, Edward. *When Parents Die*. Penguin Books, 1987.

Schiff, Harriet Sarnott. *The Bereaved Parent*. Crown Publishing, 1977.

Wylie, Betty Jane. *Beginnings: A Book for Widows*. McClelland and Stewart, 1985.

Books of general interest

Becker, Ernest. *The Denial of Death*. Macmillan, 1973.

Glaser, Barney and Strauss, Anselm. *Awareness of Dying*. Aldine Publishing, 1965.

Harpur, Tom. *For Christ's Sake*. Oxford University Press, 1986.

Hinton, John. *Dying*. Penguin Books, 1967.

Kübler-Ross, Elisabeth. *On Death and Dying*. Tavistock Publications, 1970.

Pincus, Lily. *Death and the Family: The Importance of Mourning*. Faber, 1974.

Rando, Theresa. *Grief, Dying and Death*. Research Press Company, 1984.

Worden, J. William. *Grief Counselling and Grief Therapy*. Springer, 1982.

Index